Return of the
GENTLEMAN

Return of the

GENTLEMAN

Creating Nurturing Connections *by* Embracing *the* Authentic You

Dr. Dain Heer

Access Consciousness
Publishing

Return of the Gentleman

ISBN: 978-1-63493-189-2 (trade paperback)
ISBN: 978-1-63493-193-9 (e-book)

For questions, please contact:
Access Consciousness Publishing
406 Present Street
Stafford, TX 77477
USA
accessconsciousnesspublishing.com

Cover photo: Allannah Avelin
Editors: Katarina Wallentin, Heather Nichols and Teresa Stenson

CONTENTS

GRATITUDE

This book is not my book. It is the creation of many, many gentlemen and women that have been, and are, in my life. Please know, I am so grateful for your amazing contributions.

Let me start with Gary Douglas, my best friend and business partner, a true gentleman who has been a co-discoverer of everything this book presents as a possibility. Mr. Douglas, you are the once and forever gentleman. I lift my hat in honor of your greatness!

In addition, I have some amazing gentleman in my life that I am honored to call friends. How did I get so lucky? Thank you for being. Some of you were intimately involved in creating the project that lead to this book. Liam Bramley, Brendon Watt, Connor Hill and Greame Croskill, I am so grateful for your vulnerability and courage in diving into this area together with me, friends!

Also, this book would never have come about without three phenomenal writers who took my words and made them shine. Thank you, Katarina Wallentin, Teresa Stenson and Heather Nichols. You are brilliant, ladies.

Last but definitely not least, thank you for you, my brave and courageous individual, who is about to endeavor to explore the true possibilities of being a gentleman. Together, we are the change and the gift this world requires.

YOUR INVITATION

Yes, you are invited. In whatever way you came to be reading these words on this page right at this moment, I am so happy you are here.

I'm going to go out on a limb: *I think you're reading this because you know that deep down, there's something else out there for you.*

You might have been looking for this book for a while. You might have done a little (or a lot) of research about how to be a man in this reality, and you might be frustrated and irritated because most of the materials you found do not sit right with you, and the ideas and voices behind those materials don't speak to you.

You're not interested in dominating women, or men, or the planet. The YouTube tutorials about how to get women to have sex with you are not even close to what you are looking for. The "Me-Too" campaign that started early 2018 just amplifies the total craziness that has been created in this area for both men and women.

Okay—you might want to have sexual connections with women, or men—whatever your preference, and being sexual is certainly part of being a gentleman. It's certainly something we'll cover in the book, but that's not the starting point, and it's seriously not the end goal, at all.

And I think you sense deep down that your worth as a man is not determined by how many people you can get to sleep with you. Does this sound like you?

My friend, you are a seeker (also known as a horse-person, also known as a humanoid—but we'll come back to that) and you are in exactly the right place.

Imagine This

Imagine waking up tomorrow, looking in the mirror and liking the man who is looking back at you. Liking your whole self with your whole heart. No more feelings of inferiority.

Valuing yourself. Honoring yourself. Trusting yourself. Being grateful for you: the greatness that you are, just by being you.

Feel it. Feel the burden of pleasing others lift from your shoulders. Feel all notions of *should* and *supposed-to* leave you. Feel the simplicity and the lightness of you without all of that.

In this new, lighter way of being, you no longer have to cut parts of yourself off just to fit in. You no longer need to play a role in the desperate hope that those you're attracted to will desire you.

You no longer need to keep people, including other guys, at arm's length to seem macho, or to keep some of your strength.

You no longer live in judgment—of anyone, and certainly not of the guy looking back at you in the mirror. Sounds pretty cool, right? And pretty far away, selfish and impossible.

It's okay to doubt. You're still here. You're still choosing to read. This whole process starts with a choice. When you are willing to choose something different, an abundance of doors open up to you. It is as simple and as beautiful as that.

So, here's the question: Are you are willing to open the first door, and take that step into the unknown? Or wait—is it really the unknown we're stepping into, or could it be the known?

We are, after all, *returning* to being gentlemen. I like to see us as renaissance men. Recovering, re-discovering, and re-inventing our real selves is like recovering and rediscovering long-forgotten beautiful and brilliant artifacts that have always been available. We're just shaking off whatever misidentifications and misapplications we've been lost in and letting ourselves out into the light again.

I invite you to recognize it. I invite you to choose it. I invite you to stand by my side and walk through this door together, in ease, and joy and glory—and with the elegance of a true gentleman.

I am so grateful that you are here!

Girls Allowed

While it's true that this book is called *Return of the Gentleman*, and while it's true that I'm writing it with male seekers in mind, I really don't want to exclude any female readers. Exclusion creates separation, and that's the opposite of what this book is about.

When I started talking about the issues around being a gentleman in a series of YouTube videos, I was really blown away and excited to get feedback not just from other guys, but from female viewers too. Turns out, they really got something out of watching the videos and listening to the discussions we had. I even heard from women who hadn't watched the videos, but whose partners had—and great, positive shifts were occurring in their relationships as a result.

So please, if you don't identify as a man, but you are interested in what might be going on for the men in your life right now—join us, and explore with us. You have nothing to lose, and you'll certainly gain a deeper understanding of your partner, lover, son, brother, father or friend. You might even be able to contribute to their life by sharing these ideas with them—or even better—passing this book on to them, and giving them the opportunity to discover the ideas, and these new possibilities, for themselves.

In the spirit of inclusion and difference, this is not a book aimed only at men who want to sleep with women. Part of being a gentleman is about being sexual, and the guidance in this book supports any (consenting and legal) sexual encounters you choose to have and be present in.

If you find me using gender-specific language that doesn't fit with your situation, please know it's just for the sake of brevity and that *all preferences* are honored here.

The Truth of Being a Man

If you get nothing else out of this book, please let this one possibility in: *The truth always makes you feel lighter. A lie makes you feel heavier.*

Just a few moments ago, I asked you to imagine looking in the mirror and liking the man before you. I asked you to imagine letting go of all of your thoughts about what you *should* do as a man, how you *should* act, who other people think you are *supposed to* be. You let go of all of that and you felt lighter, because it was true for you, *right* for you. And you chose to read on.

Know this: you have an instinct for what is right for you. It has just been conditioned and practiced out of you. Whether you realize it or not, you decided long ago that certain things are right for you, while other things are not, and you've never thought to stop and ask where those ideas are from, and who they belong to. The result of being in what is essentially a state of autopilot is . . . even more limitations on you.

So, I invite you to add this oh-so simple question to your gentleman's toolbox: **Light or heavy?**

Use it when an idea is presented to you in this book. Especially one that speaks to you, or one that stirs up feelings in you. Does it feel light or heavy? It's a wonderful and dynamic shortcut to knowing whether that idea is true for you.

If You Got This Far, You're Probably a Horse

We've established you're a seeker. You're looking for more. And though you are by no means alone in this, my friend, you probably already have the feeling that not everyone else is like you. You probably already sense that you're a little different than some of the people you have in your life, whether they're directly in your life, like your friends and family, or whether they're the people you catch glimpses of as they give opinions on TV, on panel shows, in newspapers, or on social media.

And though the world is made up of a myriad of people, and though difference is something to be celebrated, here's a comparison from the animal kingdom to help you understand who you are and why you are (and why you feel so different).

Those other folks—who may be (or seem to be) happy to remain stationary and accept everything they are told, who live in a passive state, chewing their cud, awaiting their fate, are like cows.

You, with your sense of adventure, with your curious mind and your capacity for change, are more akin to a horse. Two separate species, living on the same planet, each doing their own thing.

But I don't want to keep referring to people like you and I as horses (though I actually wouldn't mind it myself), and I don't want to label everyone who isn't like us as a cow. It's just a simple way to demonstrate those differences you may have been experiencing, but didn't quite know how to articulate.

Let's use two different terms. If you feel a sense of connection with how I described the traits of the horse, then you could say that like me, you're a humanoid.

And everyone else, happy with the status quo, happy to stay where they are, can keep on being regular humans.

Which one are you? Are you ready to change the status quo of what it means to be a man? *If yes, let's go!*

Part One

Finding the Gentleman Within

CHAPTER 1

___

WHAT IS A GENTLEMAN?

What I'm about to say may surprise you, or even disappoint you. You might think it's counterintuitive, ridiculous, outrageous, and so despicable that you immediately demand a refund.

But here it is: *Even though this book is about being a gentleman, I am <u>not</u> going to give you a definition of what a gentleman is.* There is no specific Dain Heer way of being a gentleman.

That would be too static, too conclusive, too prescriptive. As I have said many times, in all of my books, and most of my online materials (and in my classes, and some of my conversations . . .) I don't have any answers for you, my friend—only questions. I'm never going to tell you what to do, and I'm never going to make any demands of you.

I'm simply inviting you to explore this area with me. And to explore, we need to move away from black and white, good and bad, right and wrong ways of thinking.

A core element of this book, and a necessary step on the way to becoming a true gentleman, centers on un-defining and breaking down the roles that we feel we need to play out as men, so I'm really not going to prescribe another way for you to be.

Instead, I'd like to present you with possibilities that will get you to the place where you can be the greatest version of yourself as a man—whatever that looks like for you.

In fact, if I had to sum up what being a gentleman means in one sentence, that sentence would come pretty close.

Let me say that one more time: *Being a true gentleman is about being the greatest you can be as a man—whatever that looks like for you.*

Why Is This Conversation Required

There are so many reasons why I believe this conversation is essential right now.

First, there's the fact that it sprung from the seed of a conversation with a dear friend, which grew into a video series on YouTube, which in turn spoke to so many guys and opened up so many questions and contributions from men all over the world. Men were listening, interacting and responding. They were saying, *Yes*. And, as I said a few pages ago, so were their partners.

Let's talk more about that seed planted by that dear friend: 23-year-old Liam. He and I were discussing the different aspects of what it is to be a man. *Could a man be kind while also being powerful? Could he be vulnerable while also being sexual?*

By the way, that kind of conversation—which was open, honest and supportive—is exactly the kind of conversation men should be able to have with each other, and this is something we'll get to later in the book.

But there we were, and there Liam was, standing in front of me, saying that the very fact that we were talking in this way, about this subject, was a huge deal for him. We were covering and exploring an area which he'd struggled to find good, useful, authentic information on.

He'd scoured YouTube. He'd Googled just about every variant of the phrase, *How to be a man,* and he'd plowed through the articles and tutorials and opinion pieces that came back. He was no clearer, and no closer, to knowing how to live as the man he wanted to be in this world.

What was really lacking for Liam were resources which spoke to a possibility where being a man means you can be honorable, kind and caring *and also* potent and sexual.

Everything that this young seeker had found was *either/or*:

> You can **either** be an alpha male, **or** you can be a doormat.
>
> You can dominate a woman, or she can dominate you.

No in-betweens. No grey areas. No room for a different possibility.

And—crucially—almost all of these resources centered around getting women to like you, or to agree to sleeping with you. Like that is all there is. Like, that's how you measure your worth.

So there, in that moment, in that conversation, Liam realized it wasn't a case of *either/or*. He could be kind and strong; vulnerable and sexual; nurturing and powerful.

He could be all of those things, and so much more. And I thought, "*Well, if this curious and brilliant young man hasn't been able to find the guidance that he needs for this subject, then we need to create a platform to talk about it.*"

So, I ran a series of discussions and Q&As on YouTube, and I called it, *Return of the Gentlemen*. And, as I said earlier, men responded, women responded, and the seed of this book was planted.

If a Tree Falls in the Forest...

One of the other big indications for me that this discussion is important comes from the fact that if you happen to identify as female in this world, and you happen to want to know how to live in your power as a woman (and why wouldn't you?!) there are heaps of materials available to you. There's an abundance of amazing voices speaking to female seekers about being the greatness that they are.

I love it, and I support it, and I'm so happy those voices are here and they are being heard. They absolutely should be.

But, where are the equally authentic and empowering voices standing alongside that message for guys? Well, we've already established that they are totally outnumbered by the voices shouting, **"Getting laid is what being a real man is all about!"**

And what's the result of this imbalance? What if, like Liam, and like me, and like millions of other humanoid men, the number of people you've slept with has nothing to do with your self-worth? What if *you* are the valuable product?

If you are a man, chances are that you don't feel that you're enough. For so many (men *and* women), men are *less than*; wrong for wanting more, wrong for wanting something else, and just plain wrong!

So, we make ourselves a little smaller. Because we don't want to be that guy—that obnoxious guy taking what he wants from whomever he wants. We want to respect, nurture, and love the women in our life.

But, here we get a little confused. Here, we think that to honor a woman, we need to be less than her. We think that we need to be wrong, so she can be right.

When you see it like that—do you see how messed up it is? Ask yourself: **If a tree falls in the forest and nobody is around, is the man still wrong?**

Okay, so that's a joke (or a philosophical question, however you want to look at it) but it really speaks to me and a lot of other guys I've talked about this with, because we can have this tendency to feel that, as men, we are wrong all the time.

I would really like to get us all away from that so we can be our real, authentic selves, because when you are that guy, fully standing in his power—there's no shame, no wrongness, no being less-than. You don't need to apologize just for existing.

Separation from You

Do you see how that *either/or* way of viewing what a guy can be has totally led you astray and totally taken you away from being the greatness that you are? After all, you've been separated, not just from your true self, but from others—both men and women.

A huge part of the resources for humanoid women are about claiming their femininity and their feminine power, while the (how-to-get-laid) messages for men apparently speak to some idea of what it is to be masculine. However misguided that may be.

And the effect of all of this labeling of masculine versus feminine characteristics really just creates separation.

What if you could have it all? What if you had the so-called masculine strength to call bullshit on bullshit when you needed to, but then something more traditionally seen as feminine allows you to let it go? It doesn't become a fight, or a battle, but you have the courage to say it in the first place. Only it's not even courage, it's just you being you.

That's where I want to get us to. Where your vulnerability *is* your potency, and you have the joy of being everything that you are as a true gentleman.

Where Are We Returning From?

Remember in the invitation to this book, I said we were like renaissance people, uncovering who we really are? We're removing layers of crap from our true selves. From the gentlemen we are and can be.

So—where have you been? You've been buried under the roles you've been expected to play, by the separation as a result of all that, by the difference you are and the wrongness you feel about everything because of that, and by the way you've suppressed what is true while somewhere YOU KNOW that there must be more out there for you.

Well, are you ready for something different? Is it time to be you, no matter what? Shall we say hello to you—to the brilliant, unique elegant and potent gentleman you truly are?

Where Are We Headed?

So, now that we've skimmed the surface of where you've been, and what got you there, let me tell you where I'd like for us to get to, as a result of this conversation, and as a result of you reading this book.

If I could choose one thing for you to receive from this conversation, it would be this. (And I've already asked you to imagine it, and you may have already glimpsed the possibility of it, but here it is again.)

I would love for you to be able to look in the mirror and really like the man looking back at you.

Okay, so 'really like' sounds a little vague. Let's expand it. Really liking yourself happens when you have no shame and feel no need to apologize for who you are. It comes from honoring and valuing you. It comes from existing in a place of zero judgment. It comes from allowing yourself to be the best version of you.

And the amazing thing is, once you are at that point within yourself, all kinds of phenomenal things happen in your relationships with others. This brings me to another thing I wish for you:

I would love for you to break down the separations you have experienced with other people—both men and women—and live in a state of oneness, not just with yourself, but with those around you.

Now, that might sound like a pretty big ask. It might sound far away. You might have had a little resistance to that statement—and it might be the word 'oneness' that did it.

But really when I say that, what I'm talking about is getting us to a place where we can stand beside each other with ease—and especially where we as men can stand alongside other men—because I see so much separation and competitiveness among men. I would love to get us to a place where we can be supportive and grateful for each other.

So, as a consequence of valuing and liking yourself, others value and like you too. When you value you, separation breaks down, barriers come down, and you get to have the most wonderful connections with the rest of the world.

How Did I Get Here?

In that conversation with Liam, which kick-started this whole discussion, he told me that, from his point of view, I am a true gentleman. Somehow, just by being myself, I showed him how he could exist as a man in this world. Hearing this came as a surprise—but a really nice one—because it just wasn't something I'd given a lot of thought to at that point.

I don't see myself as a role model or as a guru of any kind, but in the spirit of sharing, I can tell you how I got to where I am now, in a place where I can say that when I look in the mirror, I really do like the man looking back at me.

I'm by no means perfect, and let me tell you, it was a long journey to get here. It did not come easy, and in many ways I am still a work in progress, but hey, we all are, and it's a thing to celebrate. What if there is no destination but the adventure of living and being you right now?

Let me tell you a little about how I got to where I am. Growing up, all of the messages I received told me in no uncertain terms: men are bad, women are good. Men are wrong, women are right. Men are nothing, women are everything.

Those messages impacted me and imprinted on me from such a young age that I carried A LOT of shame with me into my adult life, simply because I was male.

The only way I could make up for that shame, the only way I could make amends to the world and appease some of the suffering my gender had inflicted on women throughout history, was to elevate women, do all I could to ensure their happiness, and make sure their needs were met way above and beyond my own.

It wasn't until I found Access Consciousness and met Gary Douglas that I became aware of what a distorted view I had, and how I really needed to start honoring myself before I could have real, authentic and meaningful connections with others.

I had cut so many parts of myself off to please the women in my life that I was more like a shell of what I could actually be. I had to ask myself: *What would make me happy? How can I value myself?* It was the start of a continuous search, and it was the beginning of really liking myself.

Now, I'm beyond happy to tell you I am more 'me' every day, and I now have amazing relationships, friendships, and connections with an abundance of people, men and women, and most importantly, this includes the man in the mirror.

You Are Here

I am standing by your side as a fellow gentleman and saying: *Here's where we are right now as men in this reality—and here's why. And in front of us is a doorway, and through this doorway is a new way for us to be.*

If you choose to open this door with me, and take a look at what's there, then that's awesome. And if you choose to not go there—for whatever reason—then that's okay too. No judgment here, not ever.

These new ways of seeing yourself in the world might not be for you, or they might not be for you *yet*. You might find yourself coming back to the book at a future date, or you might put it down forever—that's your call.

Or, here's a third option—*some* of this stuff might be for you. Not all of it, but some of it. You might find that you feel a sense of lightness around a couple of the ideas. You might ask yourself, just as I suggested, is this light or heavy for me?

You get to choose what works. How cool is that?! How empowering is that? And how *easy* is that? Are you ready for an adventure?

CHAPTER 2

OUT WITH THE SUPPOSED MAN

I have a question for you. (I actually have a lot of questions for you. This book is overflowing with them. Unapologetically.) Anyway—here it is: **What if the biggest obstacle keeping you from being the greatness that you are is the fact that you are pretending to be someone you are not?**

Just take a moment to consider that. How does it feel? Light or heavy? How does the idea that you might be playing a part, or a role, in your life rather than living as you, feel to you? Is it a possibility?

That's all for now. We will come back to that question soon enough.

Letting Go

In this first part of our journey, I'd like to invite you to explore ideas around role-playing, and how, as a man, you may feel you have to put on an act, play a part, be someone else—just to meet external expectations (and maybe some internal ones too).

If you choose to join me, I'd like you to get to a point where you can identify if you are playing a role in any of the relationships in your life, and invite you to see how playing certain roles may be obstructing your capacity to be YOU.

When you are aware of the roles that are holding you back, you can choose something different. When you choose beyond the roles that are holding you back, you begin to be a true gentleman in the world.

Should and Supposed To

There are two phrases which are really useful to help you identify whether you are playing a role, or whether you are being you.

Allow me to introduce you to **should,** and his very good friend, **supposed to**. Think about it . . . How often do you use these words? *I should do this. I'm supposed to do that.*

Do those phrases create a lightness in your world at all? Or a sense of obligation? When you are operating from what you (or the people in your life) think you 'should' do—or are 'supposed to' do—how much freedom do you have?

What if a true gentleman can play any role and be anything, but from his own choice and sense that it would create something greater, rather than from expectation or obligation?

When you show up in the world according to the expectations of other people in your life, as well as your own, you are being a doormat rather than a true gentleman.

Basically, you keep yourself in a very small box.

Say Hello to Choice and Space

When you are functioning from all of the roles you think you are supposed to play for other people, in order to be a 'good' partner, parent, employee, or a man in the world, you lose one of the most essential aspects of being a gentleman: question and choice.

What if you started to ask the following three questions for...well...EVERYTHING?

What would create the most here?

What would I like to create?

What would a true gentleman choose to be and do here?

There is no space for you to be the greatness that you are if you believe you don't have the choice to be anything outside of the roles you are playing.

There is no space for you to be the greatness that you are if you're trapped in a box of other people's (or your own) expectations.

What if being a gentleman is not about showing up the way people want you to? What if being a gentleman is about showing up in the world and in your relationships in a way that will always create something greater—for others, as well as for you? And what if that can look different in every situation?

When you can choose what is going to work for you, you become empowered, you have more fun, and your relationships can become greater too!

Time to Introduce Some Magic

In the same way that this whole journey to being a gentleman is an invitation, I would like to invite you to use, or at least get to know, the Access Consciousness clearing statement.

The clearing statement is, well, exactly what its name suggests. It is a statement, or a set of words, that you can say to clear the path in front of you and to let go of what might be limiting or defining you, and keeping you stuck. In other words, rather than just looking at your points of view that have limited you and hoping that changes them, you are actively CHANGING THEM.

It is possible that in trying to find your way as a man in this world you have placed certain limits (and expectations, projections and judgments) on yourself, and these limits are getting in the way of you becoming the man you truly are.

If you allow it to, the clearing statement can play a key part in setting you free from those limiting beliefs—even the ones you may not know you are carrying—by destroying and uncreating them. The amazing thing is, once those beliefs dissolve, the way is clear for new possibilities and experiences in your life.

Once again, rather than just looking at your points of view that have limited you, and hoping that changes them, you are actively CHANGING THEM.

I know, it is not supposed to be that easy. I thought the same thing too the first time I heard about this clearing statement. What if this is actually what is required and now available to you?

You have nothing to lose by trying it, and possibly your entire life to gain.

A Closer Look

This is the clearing statement: ***Right and wrong, good and bad, POD & POC, all 9, shorts, boys and beyonds.***

I can just imagine your expression if you're reading that for the first time . . . you probably went, "What?!"

There's a good chance your brain feels a little fried from what appears to be a random set of words. It really helps to look at the clearing statement in context, so here's one in action.

This is actually from Chapter 1 of this book, and it's the first instance of a clearing statement that I'll invite you to use.

What have I made so vital, valuable, and real about living from the box of other peoples' expectations that keeps me from being the greatness of the gentleman I truly be? Everything that is, times a godzillion, will you destroy and uncreate it please? **Right and wrong, good and bad, POD & POC, all 9, shorts, boys and beyonds.**

Note how there is always a question before the clearing statement. The question is always the start of the process, and it's where we open our beings to the possibility of change: they bring out the very energy that is in the way of change. Functioning from the question in this way keeps us out of conclusion and judgment and allows new ways of functioning into our lives.

The thing is, to get to the new we need to clear out the old. We need to undo (or destroy) and uncreate the outdated and restrictive conclusions, limitations, judgments, thoughts, feelings and emotions that we have bought into, usually without even being aware of it.

That's what the clearing statement does. Can you see the double-whammy nature of it? If we choose it, it can undo what doesn't serve us, AND it can clear the way for more of what we truly want, who we truly are, and what really makes us happy.

This clearing statement is one of the keys to the kingdom if you've ever wanted to create lasting change in your limited points of view and kick them to the curb forever.

So what do these words actually mean?

Right and wrong, good and bad, POD & POC, all 9, shorts, boys and beyonds.

The truth is, you don't need to understand every element of the clearing statement, but I know you'll try, and that's okay, it means you're curious and you're interested in change and progress. That's why you are here, exactly here, right now.

On top of that, our minds have this tendency to want to know everything about a new thing, to really 'get it', to understand it, to label it, to conquer it, to know it.

The truth is, the quickest and most active way to understand the clearing statement is to use it and experience the life-changing impact of it.

Still curious? Let's break it down into three parts.

The Meaning Beyond the Words:

- **Right and wrong, good and bad**

  This stands for the judgments you are holding about whatever it is you're letting go of (what you are letting go of is in the question before the clearing statement). And yes, it's important to let go of every belief or idea you have about that thing—good or bad, right or wrong. All of it.

- **POD & POC**

  Point of destroy and point of create

  This allows us to go back in time to the point where a belief was created or destroyed. Usually we have no idea where that point is, and the beauty is we don't need to know. It just works. POD & POC is such a swift and neat way to obliterate anything that is keeping you from being the greatness that you are.

- **All 9, shorts, boys and beyonds**

  Okay, here's where your mind might do its very best to really, really, *really* know what these words mean. Briefly, **all 9** are the layers of the clearing statement. (I was part of developing those 9 layers and even I don't remember all of them. See, you don't need to know them either.)

Shorts stands for what's meaningless and meaningful about it, and all of the punishments and rewards that go with that.

Boys are the nucleated spheres—aka the layers of the onion of the thing you're trying to get to.

Beyonds is anything that has ever stopped you in your tracks, those experiences beyond thought, beyond emotion.

How's your head? It's totally fine if these words send you into a spin, I get it. But if you are willing to let them into your life, you can start creating the life you would like to choose, and that is when you, my friend, will soar.

Whenever the clearing statement pops up in the pages of this book, I invite you to take the time to read it and to say it out loud. Or you can just say it in your head if you prefer. Just try it. Just try and see if it changes something. Because it just may.

Remember, the clearing statement is **a tool for change**. A way to destroy and uncreate anything which doesn't serve us, which keeps us stuck, which limits or defines us.

Let's Try it Out on Our Roles

Here, in this moment of this chapter, we're concerned with letting go of any roles we have been trying to play which are keeping us from being the greatness that we are. If you're open to it, read this statement out loud, and see how it feels for you:

What have I made so vital, valuable, and real about living from the box of other peoples' expectations that keeps me from being the greatness of the gentleman I truly be? Everything that is, times a godzillion, will you destroy and uncreate it please? **Right and wrong, good and bad, POD & POC, all 9, shorts, boys and beyonds.**

Just repeat that (out loud if possible) until the energy starts to shift.

Now ask yourself, "*Is there more space for me to be me?*" This, my friends, is the beginning of a totally different possibility for being a gentleman.

Why Do We Play Roles?

Let's start with the obvious, the surface-level stuff about why we might find ourselves in a place where we've taken on a particular role in one or many of our relationships.

We've established that playing a role has a lot to do with expectations. We understand that we may modify our behavior, or even pretend to be someone else entirely, just to live up to other people's expectations, and to fit in their box.

Somewhere, somehow, a connection has been made where we equate not fitting into someone else's box with letting them down, being unkind, and not respecting them.

We think if we were our full self, if we let it all out, really exhaled and let our gorilla get comfortable, we'd be selfish, and someone who doesn't care for or respect others.

Excuse me— who are you calling a gorilla???

Oops—I introduced him too early. Don't worry, we'll come back to him. But, seriously, one of the most uncaring and disrespectful things we can do to ourselves is get in that box and stay there. It is more destructive to fit into that box than to flatten it or crush it.

The most destructive thing you can do is try to be something you are not. **But ... bombshell moment ...**

It's not just other people's boxes we force ourselves into; it's our own too. The box you are squashed into may actually have been constructed by you.

Just consider that. Here it is again: **The box you are squashed into may actually have been constructed by you.**

Check how this feels: light or heavy? You may be playing a role or assuming a particular identity in your life because at some point you decided or concluded— perhaps not cognitively— that it's what other people expect of you, and it's what you expect of yourself.

What happens if you don't play a role you decided you ought to play? Well, at first, you might feel like a failure, and all other kinds of wrong. And why? Because, chances are, my friend, you are living in judgment of yourself.

We're going to talk more about judgment and how to get out of it in Chapter 2, but for now it's enough to consider the possibility that you may be playing some of the roles in your relationships because you decided to, and because you'll judge yourself as a failure if you don't.

So, I said I'd come back to the gorilla. He weighs 800 lbs. and he's squashed into a box that is far, far too small for him.

He's cramped, he's uncomfortable, and he has no room to be himself. He might have even had to cut parts of himself off just to fit. (Weird when you think he might have helped construct that box himself, isn't it?)

Let's take a look at some of the boxes that we, as men, in this reality, have tried to fit ourselves into, but this time we're focusing on the roles we've played purely in the relationships we've had with women, or whomever we are attracted to.

But first: *Caution!* I've said this already but I'll say it again: being a gentleman is not another role for you to play. There is a strong chance I will remind you about this again before the end of the book.

The key word here is, *being*. **Being a gentleman.** Not playing at being a gentleman. Not pretending that you are a gentleman, while secretly believing you are not. It's about being the best you can be as a man in this world, whatever that looks like for you.

Don't worry if that feels too vague or far-off right now.

Some Typical Boxes

Let's go back to that conversation I had with my friend Liam that kick-started this whole movement around returning to being a gentleman. Liam, like so many of you, felt stranded.

He wanted guidance on how to be a man in this reality, and when he looked for advice, all he found were tips on how to get women to sleep with him, and how to dominate women. Namely: how to be the alpha male. Things like: *How to Become an Alpha Male: 13 Steps (with Pictures)* or *How to Be an Alpha Male: Ten Traits of the Modern-Day Alpha.*

A look in a dictionary says that an alpha male is someone *"tending to assume a dominant or domineering role in social or professional situations"* and that *"most alpha males need to control the women in their lives."*

But, what if you are not interested in domination and control over women? What if you are interested in a different way of being with them and the world that is about kindness and being a gentleman?

If being an alpha male is not appealing to you, and you are looking for something different, for most men the only other choice is to be the opposite: something I would call a 'SNAG' (sensitive new age guy). Here, you don't get to have testicles, and you have to be mostly at the whim of what women—and the world—want from you.

What if there is something beyond the 'either or' of alpha male *or* sensitive new age guy? What If you could simply be *you*?

Let's show the phrase, "either, or" to the door once and for all. I'm not just talking about the alpha male OR the SNAG. I also invite you to get rid of notions such as...

Masculine OR Feminine.

Sexual OR Vulnerable.

Powerful OR Emotional.

Strong OR Kind.

Because...(and this next sentence is important) *judgments, conclusions and points of view always limit creation and create separation.* There is a very good chance I'll repeat this later in the book. Like right now! *Judgments, conclusions and points of view always limit creation and create separation.*

When we move away from black and white thinking (or judgments, conclusions and points of view), we move away from those sneaky places where we separate from ourselves and from each other. And when you get out of separation, you have a space of *being* that also gives you much greater access to what is true for you.

And you can be so much in that space. You can be present with your partner and you can let them know when you could use their presence, too. You can be vulnerable and potent, silly and tenacious, weird and wonderful without having to fit a defined role of who you can and can't be in any given moment.

So, my friend, let me ask you: *Are you willing to let go of those roles that are not at all the product of an empowered choice?*

More specifically... *Time for a New Role?*

I get that it can be scary to let go of a role you have been playing for a long time. But, all I am inviting you to do is to get to a place where you are open to something else, to another way of being.

By opening yourself up to the possibility of letting go of any roles which are holding you back, you will create that space and freedom around you, where wonderful, amazing changes occur. Things that right now seem far away, and impossible, start here.

If you are willing to choose it.

If you are willing to let go of pretending, should, and supposed-to's.

If you are willing to go beyond judgments, conclusions and points of view.

If you are open to having all the space you need to be your greatest self.

Guess what? I have a few more questions for you. You might never have asked yourself these kinds of questions before. Just see what comes up for you:

If it were up to me, what would I like to choose?

How would I like to be?

How would I like to show up in the world?

The 800lb Gorilla

When you allow yourself to be the 800lb gorilla in the room, you take up all the space you need as all of you. It's not about being the biggest, strongest, most muscled guy—because when you are being you, you don't have to use force, or be intimidating to get your point across.

Whether you're 800lb or 100lb, when you are being you, you dissolve the boxes and boundaries around you, the world changes around you as a result, and you begin to be the greatest "you" you can be.

And how do you know? Well for one, you begin to have admiration and gratitude when you look at that guy in the mirror. **You.**

But … what about the women?

"Pssst, Dain, Dain—this is really great and yeah, I'm totally on-board for choosing something different, but please will you just tell me—what kind of man do women really want?"

My friend and fellow seeker, yes, I do understand why you might want to know this. Here is the Catch 22 of that question: If your main purpose is to make sure you give people (some of them women) what they decided they want from you—where do YOU fit into that equation? You always end up in second place.

It puts you in a state of *should*. It brings up a whole load of supposed-to's. **It's the beginning of cutting *you* off from you since what becomes vital is *all those other people's (women's) needs*.**

Try this instead: flip it around. Instead of thinking about *how you should be* in order for women to find you attractive, consider how you *would like to be* in the world, and when you are being that, who will find you attractive? Who will find you valuable, who will want to be around you, when you are being how you would like to be?

Tap into the awareness of something different. Tap into that space—that is enough. ***You* are enough.** Besides, if you choose what is true for you, you will naturally be more attractive and more potent.

Once you start to embrace new possibilities, amazing things happen. It's like a domino effect—something new will come into your world, and that new thing will have more possibility and consciousness to it, and then your choices expand, and what you can be gets greater, and what you can contribute changes too! Just like that.

Oh, and you may also get happier!

CHAPTER 3

HONOR WHO YOU TRULY ARE

Whenever you decide to make a change, or have more of something in your life, the quickest way to get traction with that change is to identify where you are already *being* the change now. Well, what if you are already being it?

Ask yourself, *"Where in my life am I already being a gentleman?"*

You might want to get specific. Think of what being a gentleman means to you. Does it involve being kind? Standing up for yourself? Feeling relaxed in the company of whomever you're with? Let's just take one of those traits now: kindness. Have you ever:

Treated someone with kindness?
Honored those who have come across your path?
Contributed to another person's day in a positive way?

Maybe you were behind someone at the grocery store who didn't have quite enough money to pay for their shopping. They'd miscalculated the value of the items in their basket and were all set to put some of them back when you said, "Hey—it's okay—I'll get that," and you paid the difference.

Or, perhaps you spent time talking to the new guy at work because he seemed a little nervous in his first week. Or, you saw someone struggling with a heavy bag and you offered to carry it for them. Or, you were eating alone in a restaurant and instead of getting annoyed with the stressed-out mom at the next table as she wrestled with her screaming toddler, you gave her a smile.

These are all ways you may have been a positive, kind and honoring presence in someone else's life, and if you see kindness as a gentlemanly quality, then these are all ways you are already showing up as a gentleman in this world.

One of the biggest difficulties for us as guys is that we're in a constant state of judgment of ourselves for not being enough. So, take a moment to acknowledge the times when you have been more than enough.

Expansion happens when we acknowledge where we already are.

It's such a quick, easy, simple, straightforward and effective way for you to start to see very real results on your quest to become—*or return to being*—a gentleman. **Simply**: acknowledge something and you will see it grow.

Honoring Is the Key

If I had to choose one word to sum up this whole process, or suggest one thing for you to be as a gentleman, it would be honoring, because a huge part of being a gentleman involves honoring others.

This means honoring both the women and men in your life, and—if you have them—your children. It's also about honoring your commitments to others as well as our future on this planet. But, none of that is possible until you honor . . . (you know what's coming, don't you?)

YOU

So, let's take a look at what is arguably the most important relationship you will ever have: **the one with yourself.**

Having allowance, gratitude, and honoring for yourself all form the foundations of being a true gentleman. And, here's a little side-note. If you do feel like the idea of having a relationship with yourself is a feminine thing, you might want to start asking: *"Who does this belong to?"*

Often, when we think something trips our trigger, it is actually just where we are aware of everybody else around us and their points of view. What would an honoring relationship with you be like? Would it create more space and ease in your world? If that makes you feel lighter, then you are simply just very aware, my friend, of everybody else's points of view.

How many points of view that having a great relationship with you is a wrongness have you bought from others? Everything that is, times a godzillion, will you destroy and uncreate it please? **Right and wrong, good and bad, POD & POC, all 9, shorts, boys and beyonds.**

By the way, a "godzillion" is a number so big, only God knows. It's like steroids for the clearing statement.

Whose lies and what lies have you bought about what being a man (and a gentleman) really means? Everything that is, times a godzillion, will you destroy and uncreate it please? **Right and wrong, good and bad, POD & POC, all 9, shorts, boys and beyonds.**

Whose lies and what lies are you using to create the wrongness of having a close relationship with you as a man? _Everything that is, times a godzillion, will you destroy and uncreate it please?_ **Right and wrong, good and bad, POD & POC, all 9, shorts, boys and beyonds.**

Whose lies have you bought and what lies are you using to create your confusion about what it means to be a man (and a gentleman) in this world? Everything that is, times a godzillion, will you destroy and uncreate it please? **Right and wrong, good and bad, POD & POC, all 9, shorts, boys and beyonds.**

What have you made so vital, valuable and real about this reality's definition of masculinity that you see any sign, display or embrace of the sensitive part of you as a wrongness, weakness or a threat to your very being as a man? Everything that is, times a godzillion, will you destroy and uncreate it please? **Right and wrong, good and bad, POD & POC, all 9, shorts, boys and beyonds.**

While I'm not into defining what a gentleman is, I will say that honoring yourself is how it all starts. And that involves letting go of who you're not—those roles we looked at in Chapter 1—and embracing who you are.

Another trap that people sometimes fall into—men and women alike—is thinking that it's selfish, weak, or indulgent to have a healthy and honoring relationship with yourself. I assure you, my friend, it is none of those things. It's the gateway to greatness, and the foundation of being a gentleman. Still a little resistance? Try this.

<u>Whose lies have you bought and what lies have you bought from others that loving and respecting yourself is selfish, indulgent or weak? Everything that is, times a godzillion, will you destroy and uncreate it please?</u> **<u>Right and wrong, good and bad, POD & POC, all 9, shorts, boys and beyonds.</u>**

If you want to be honored, appreciated and valued by those around you, I invite you to be that for yourself first. Be you and change the world. Honor, appreciate, nurture and value yourself and others will follow, I guarantee it.

When I first came to Access, I was so far away from being a guy who honored himself, and I was completely oblivious to it. Gary Douglas did a great job of opening my eyes to the fact that I was so determined to honoring everyone else, especially in my relationships with women, that I totally disregarded and neglected honoring myself. In fact, you know that notion of cutting off parts to fit into boxes that I spoke about in Chapter 1? That was me. I was a total cut-job.

I repeatedly chose to be with women because I thought I could make them happy. Like that was my only goal: make her happy. Then, when she wasn't happy, this was me: *Okay, here's my arm. Let me cut off my arm for you.*

It took me quite some time to realize the cutting thing didn't work. The women I had relationships with were never any happier when I cut parts of myself off. But before I came to that realization, I just thought I needed to keep doing what I was doing, only better, and on a bigger, more dramatic scale: *Okay, I'll cut off my leg! That's bigger than an arm so it should keep you happy forever. Oh wait—that only lasted ten minutes!*

Eventually I got to the point where I knew I needed to do something different. Fundamentally different. *Fundamentally . . . different.* Or FFD. You can choose which word is missing.

So, I switched things around. I took that step toward honoring myself. For the first time ever I asked: *What would make me happy?* And at last, the answer wasn't: *to make her happy.* Or anyone else, for that matter. And, as I said in the introduction to this book, it was the start of a continuous search, and it was the start of me really getting to like myself.

I asked you a set of questions in Chapter 1. Let me take that one step further.

> *If I were being me, and a gentleman, who would I be?*
> *If I were being me, and a gentleman, when would I be?*
> *If I were being me, and a gentleman, what would I be?*
> *If I were being me, and a gentleman, why would I be?*
> *If I were being me, and a gentleman, what would be*
> *   fun for me?*

These questions will really help you to get to the core of what is true for you, as a being and a gentleman. In fact, just giving yourself the time to explore these questions is in itself honoring you.

What Will This Create or Decay?

Being a gentleman is also about being able to recognize whether something you are doing, or are about to do, is honoring you, and if it is creating the future you truly desire. *How?* Well . . . you just *ask*. It's that easy.

> You can ask it in a straightforward way;
> *Will this [thing I am about to do] be honoring me?*
> Or, you can even break it down and get specific by
> asking:
> *Will this create a greater future? Or will it decay my*
> *   future?*
> If you're not sure, see which feels lighter. You can
> always ask again:
> *Will this choice create or decay the future you would*
> *   like to have?*

It's amazing how, just by asking this question, you will have more awareness of what is true for you, and you may even find yourself making choices to not do the thing you think you really want to do. Or, if I can be a little blunt here, *not do the person you think you really want to do.*

And I have to tell you, it took me a long, long (long) time to get to the point where I could walk away from having a potentially great time with someone who wanted to sleep with me, because I knew the experience wouldn't be honoring me, but when I did walk away— just wow! I was fully and totally honoring myself, and it was awesome!

How are you feeling about that? Are you thinking that's total madness? Can you imagine turning down the chance to have sex with someone who may very well be incredibly beautiful, just because you know that it won't contribute to your future in any way?

Well, I get it. Most of us, especially as men, have the point of view that if somebody wants to be with us, then we should really comply. We need to be the chosen one, rather than the choosing one.

But as you start this process of honoring you, you start to become the choosing one, and you make choices which you know will unfold in the best way possible for you.

Do It Anyway!

At times, even though a particular action is going to decay your future—do it anyway. *Wait, what?!*

Seriously. If there is something you want to do really, really badly, how likely is it that you will even get to a point where you ask yourself the create / decay question anyway? Maybe you'll ask it, and you'll recognize it's going to decay your future, but you'll still go ahead and do it anyway.

And that's okay. It's okay to indulge. It's okay to make a choice that will decay your future, when you are aware you're making that choice. You are aware of it, and you are willing to indulge anyway. This is very empowering, very honoring, and as such it's a very gentlemanly thing to do.

So, there you are, about to decay your future in some way. At this point, if you can take a breath, ask yourself: *How can I make this as easy as possible on me and my future? How much fun can I have doing it anyway?*

What if you could enjoy the fact that you're making a choice that will decay your future? How freaking cool are you?!

When you are willing to honor yourself, you don't make yourself wrong when you make a choice that didn't work out so well, because that's not honoring. Instead, you say, "Okay, well that didn't work out so well. What else can I choose in the future?"

By the way, how is this totally different way of being in the world feeling to you? Kind of exciting, huh?

The Joy of Messing Up

You are not perfect, nor do you need to be. Perfection is never what is required. Enjoyment of your choices and gratitude for the fact that you can choose is what's required. Even when those choices are supposedly "wrong."

What if I told you I find joy in messing up?

It's true. When I was a teenager, I had a friend called Jeff, to whom I'll always be grateful for teaching me this particular lesson: it is okay to mess up, and it is even better if you can laugh at yourself after you've messed up. Jeff taught me that, just by being it himself. He had this wonderful way of poking fun at himself, and I really admired that about him.

I was actually quite a serious kid, and when you look at the kind of upbringing I had, you can see why. I was far more responsible than any of the adults around me, including my parents, and I had this immense and heavy feeling that I had to make up for their shortcomings by looking after everything and everyone. And I did that starting at age of six years old.

So, when I met Jeff, and experienced his humor and his lightness, those qualities were awakened in me too. They had always been there—just buried under years of obligation, worry and concern.

As a side note: if you're that serious guy, it's okay. Like me, maybe you have good reason to be. Maybe you were that kid who took on too much, far more than he ever should have had to.

I invite you to choose to perceive that seriousness— which came from wanting the best for those you love— as a strength, as part of you, as a quality you have. Even when you didn't have the tools to protect everyone, you tried with all your might to keep them safe. Recognize the strength in that. Even if other people don't see your seriousness as a strength, once you do, it won't matter whether they do or not.

And, if you choose it, you can be lighter and more joyful too. Accept that sometimes you're going to mess up. We all do it.

So, what if you could enjoy it? What if you could have a good time doing it? What if you didn't have to make yourself wrong? *And what if you didn't have to try to prove you're so damn perfect anymore?*

CHAPTER 4

―――

GETTING AWAY
FROM JUDGMENT

We've looked at the ways we try to fit into other people's judgments (those boxes of expectation) and we've touched on how we might have built, or helped to build, some of those boxes ourselves.

Now, let's explore this issue of judgment in more depth, because letting go of judgment is what actually allows you to honor and value yourself in the first place!

Oh, and did I mention that when you value yourself, others value you as a direct result of that? It's worth mentioning again, just in case there are any of you still thinking that you have to be validated by others to be valuable. Nope. It starts with us. Others will follow, or not. And if they don't, does it matter?

Back to the Mirror

Right at the start of the book, I asked you to imagine waking up tomorrow, looking in the mirror and liking the man who is looking back at you. And I also told you that one of things I'd like you to get out of this whole experience is just that: genuinely liking YOU.

Let's take that a step further. Imagine looking in the mirror and being able to look at you, all of you—and having no judgments at all, "positive" or "negative." What would it be like if you could look in the mirror and make no assessments of your physical appearance, and have no opinions about any of the things you've done or the choices you have ever made?

Imagine looking in the mirror right now and having total acceptance of yourself, today, in this moment—not when you've lost 10 pounds, or when you've found your dream job, or met your ideal partner, or stopped smoking 20 a day. Just you, enjoying you, as you are, today.

Having total allowance for yourself as you are in this moment is one of the most freeing experiences you can have. It is such a relief. It is so light. Wanna try it?

Head to a mirror.

Full length if you can, phone camera if that's all you have (if you can stand in front of a mirror and have no judgment about yourself, then you're going above and beyond, my friend!) Simply look at your reflection.

Now, it's highly likely that years of conditioning are going to bring up a whole load of judgy garbage for you right away. The judgments might sound like this:

Ugh look at you!
Look at your nose
You look so tired
OMG you're old
Remember how good we looked as a teenager?

And if you're looking at your whole body:

Should you have fat there?
Shouldn't you have more fat there?
Your arms are too skinny
Didn't you have pecs once upon on time?

And so on. I could have made that list as long as this whole book because, sadly, those kinds of judgments are abundant in most peoples' minds. But maybe you're not most people, or most guys, and you're looking in the mirror and thinking:

Hey, look at you!
Have you been working out?
You have such great biceps

Yeah flex them some more!
The women freaking love you!

Well—I invite you to let go of those judgments too, because they are still judgments, even though you think you're being positive. For now, for this exercise, try to look at yourself and draw zero conclusions about how you look, or how you've ever looked, or behaved, or acted.

Try it now, and don't worry (don't judge yourself) if it's too hard, or doesn't come easily.

In fact, if doing this exercise is too much, then that's okay. It can be pretty confronting. Just consider it as a possibility for the future, that you will be able look at yourself with no judgment, even if it's just for a moment. *Not so easy?*

It's really tricky for a lot of guys to accept themselves exactly as they are because they are so used to functioning from a place of shame, guilt or wrongness.

Add into the mix all of the judgments put on them from so many directions—ways you should be, are supposed to be—ALL OF THAT—and it can seem like an impossible task to shift all of that heaviness into something different.

And if you're feeling that way, just know that it's okay, and that even if right now you don't believe you can accept yourself just as you are, I know you can. I've done it. Guys all over the world are doing it right now. We all have your back.

We're just not *on* your back, because, you know— that would make the load you've been carrying even heavier. And it has been heavy at times, hasn't it?

Why So Heavy?

Why might you, as a man in this world, have been carrying such a weight of judgment around with you? Well, that is really one of those, *"Where do we start?!"* kind of questions.

I'm just going to go broad here and start with these two big, umbrella reasons why it might be easy for you to judge yourself.

You've always been different from other guys.

Maybe that's because you're not into baseball, or soccer, or rugby, or drinking, or seeing women as inferior. I'm not saying all other guys are like that. I'm just saying that's a particular stereotype that some guys buy into, and if you are around those kinds of guys and feel like you don't fit in—there's a good chance you judge yourself as being somehow 'wrong' for that.

You've never felt like you are the kind of guy that women are attracted to, or want to be with.

You don't have the right body, or you don't make enough money, or you haven't read the right books, or you don't drive the right car. Where does all that judgment come from?

Some people (including some women) might have those points of view, but many, many do not. Sadly, we're fed these ideas about what women want from men and vice versa, and they are so far from the truth, so centered around material goods, and so likely to keep you miles away from honoring yourself. Please stop putting yourself in second place based on points of view that are not even yours.

If we look under these two umbrella reasons, we'll find thousands of other little, specific moments of judgment. And if we look closely at those, we will see even more. Suffice it to say, they are there—reasons like, 'You've always been different from your family," or "You were brought up Catholic" *(or fill in any other religions with an emphasis on judgment and guilt).*

Whenever you make a judgment about yourself, you are, in that moment, stepping out of the greatness of you. Period. You are eliminating the greatness of you in that moment. Imagine what would be possible if you didn't do that. Imagine where you could go from there.

Well, I'm Okay—But Look at This Guy!

Even if you don't say things like this out loud, do they still occur to you sometimes?

Look at his car—it's so old.
Look at that guys hair—what is up with that?
Why is he singing out loud with that voice?

And remember—we can be judgmental about positive things as well:

Wow—look at his car! It is so awesome.
How does he get his hair to do that? It looks so good.
This guy has the best voice, he should totally be a superstar.

It can be hard to see the positive remarks as judgments, but that's what they are—because you then have an ideal to measure yourself against on either side of the coin—'positive' or 'negative'. Judgment in any form never allows you to have freedom.

There will, of course, be times when you observe something, perhaps some behavior in a friend, which you know is small or less than what they are capable of being. You can be aware of that, and know they are being unkind or mediocre, <u>but you just don't have to have a point of view about it.</u>

A gentleman operates from awareness of what is possible for each and every person they are around, including themselves.

What Happens When We Stop Judging?

Amazingness. Amazingness happens.

Because once you are out of judgments, points of view and conclusions—you become the greatness of you. You begin to function from possibilities. You become a massive contribution to the world.

And...you become unstoppable, my friend. *You begin to soar!*

This is really important: *Being a gentleman is not another opportunity for self-judgment.* I know, you would so like to go there...And what if you didn't have to?

We have established that being a gentleman is not another role for you to play. Nor is it another standard for you to judge yourself against. What if you are actually far more brilliant than you realize right now?

When we get new information it's easy to judge ourselves according to that new information—and we're probably still judging us according to the old information. It's all part of that heavy load we've been carrying, and I invite you to let it all go.

It is so easy to get caught in the wheel of judgment . . .

You mess up.
You judge yourself for messing up.
Then you judge yourself for judging yourself for messing
* up.*
Then you judge yourself for judging yourself for judging
* yourself for messing up.*

And so on; never-ending. Please don't judge yourself for judging yourself. What if to judge, or not to judge, you could truly just be a choice?

What have you made so vital, valuable and real about the orders and schematics of judgment as the source for the creation of your being in this reality, that keeps you from the chaos of being the true gentleman, beyond judgment, that can invite and create a far greater reality? Everything that is, times a godzillion, will you destroy and uncreate it please? **Right and wrong, good and bad, POD & POC, all 9, shorts, boys and beyonds.**

Chaos: Where the Freedom Is

We're so used to functioning from roles, from separation, from judgments and from conclusions, that it's possible that all of this newness, however amazing it is, is bringing with it a sense of chaos for you. Morals and other people's agendas for you keep you in an ordered universe, where you don't have to worry about handling the chaos that often comes with this degree of choice and freedom.

Chaos is where the freedom is. You are letting go of your limitations, and that puts you in a state of constant movement—and what's truly awesome about movement is that it has momentum, and it is malleable and changeable. It's in a constant state of movement—or chaos—total consciousness is possible.

The boxes of reality, as you knew them, start to dissolve and you suddenly have space around you—total space to choose who you want to be, how you want to be.

What have you made so vital, valuable and real about the orders of being a man in this reality that keep you from the chaos of being the true gentleman that can and will create a far greater reality? Everything that is, times a godzillion, will you destroy and uncreate it please? **Right and wrong, good and bad, POD & POC, all 9, shorts, boys and beyonds.**

In any given moment, know that you have choices available to you. And then, the only question for you, as a gentleman, is, *"What's going to create the most?"*

Part Two

Being the Gentleman in the World

Let's take a moment to acknowledge where we are, and where we are going.

Part One of the book had its emphasis very much on us as individuals. We looked at the roles that were holding us back, started to clear some of the wrongness and judgment, and added in the key element of honoring who we really are. This lays the foundation for where we'll go next.

Part Two of the book builds on all of the above as we look at how we, as gentlemen, can create the possibilities for us to have happier, more fulfilled, and contributive relationships with those around us. Whether those relationships are sexual, platonic or familial, Part Two of the book looks at how—now that you've started to find him—you can be the gentleman that you are out in the world.

So, in this moment, consider:

From here, what else is possible? What else can I create?

CHAPTER 5

SEXUALNESS
AND POTENCY

Although I don't wish to define what a gentleman is (on two accounts: one—you are all individuals, and two—because I really don't want to give you another yardstick to measure yourself against), I would like to share with you the possibility that **a gentleman functions from sexualness.**

I'm dedicating a whole chapter to exploring this area because the idea that you can be *both* gentlemanly *and* sexual are foreign concepts in this reality, and a key piece of this entire conversation!

What Exactly Is Sexualness?

Sex is a huge and highly judged area of life for most people. The intensity of judgment around it can create a lot of confusion, because 'sex' means something totally different to everybody! For you to get clear on what is true for you with your sexual energy, identifying some of the different elements and energies of 'sex' can be extraordinarily helpful. Otherwise, you are stuck in the conversation of what it takes to get laid, and that's about as far as you can go.

Sexualness is actually a space of *being*. It is when you are alive, engaged, and connected to your body and the world. *It is healing, caring, nurturing, generative, creative, joyful, expansive, and orgasmic energies*. Notice how I didn't say anything about copulation? Copulation is something different— it is simply putting body parts together. Copulation can include the energies of sexualness, or not. Sexualness is something you can be in the world, all the time, and when you are willing to be it, it is a gift to you and to the world.

So how does a gentleman function from sexualness? Great question!

Let's dive into some potential questions you might have on the subject of sexualness and how it relates to being a gentleman.

Let's talk about sexualness and having sex.

How often is sex a caring, nurturing, expansive, joyful, creative and orgasmic experience for you? If it's not, it's often because of the intensity of judgment, shame, guilt, fear, and all kinds of other things that come with this highly charged topic.

Often, feelings of inferiority or superiority, inadequacy and wrongness abound—even if you're having sex with someone you love. If you've experienced sex like that, it's because you were functioning from *sexuality*, rather than sexualness. And there is a big difference between sexuality and sexualness.

Sexualness is a space that you be, it is an energy. Sexuality, on the other hand, is always about judgment. What? I know! (And, as always, please try this on for yourself and see if it is light for you!)

Let's look a bit closer at the idea of sexuality being about judgment. When you are functioning from sexuality, judgment is the source of your turn on. Copulation done from sexuality is about performance, proving, and getting it right (which, for most humanoids, is an immediate turn *off!*)

When we show up in the world with the energy of sexuality, we are looking to prove our value and receive validation from others that we are right, good, perfect, and correct—especially in regard to anything involving sexual energy and attractiveness.

Have you ever noticed somebody who is being so totally *them* —with no walls, no proving, total kindness—and found them to be incredibly attractive and inviting? That is a space of sexualness. Copulation done with sexualness can have many textures, and yet always includes the energies of kindness, gentleness, vulnerability, and potency. It can be a gift of expansion for both you and your partner. Moving through the world with sexualness makes you a rare, potent gentleman who is able and willing to make other people's lives greater just by being present and being YOU.

Because sexualness is an energy, when you truly embrace it and allow it to flow through you, it is actually a way of being. And despite the word 'sex' being in there, sexualness is about so much more than putting body parts together.

What else can sexualness be about, apart from sex?
When you function from sexualness, and you are free to be *you* in the world, it encompasses and affects every area of your life in phenomenal ways. You have the capacity to heal, to be caring, nurturing, expansive, joyful, creative and orgasmic.

Sexualness is like a superpower—with it, everything becomes greater. It is an energy that nurtures your life, your creations, your body, and everyone you come into contact with. Add to it orgasmic energy, the intensely pleasurable energy that creates life itself, and you become an unstoppable force in the world.

Really? Really! It's true. Great food, awesome

conversations, breath-taking views, or just that inspiring sense of possibility and openness can be orgasmic and increase the space of sexualness in your life.

But sexualness includes copulation, right? I can still have sex?

Of course, but, I promise you, if you have sex from a place of sexualness, it will blow your mind.

Where do I sign up? (You already did!) *So, how do I function from sexualness?*

First, you realize that it is there, in you, already. You were born with it, so really, it's just a case of reconnecting with it, basically switching it on again!

One of the ways you can start to function from greater sexualness is simply to ask for it! Run this:

Everything that doesn't allow the energy of true sexualness to become a reality for you, will you destroy and uncreate it, please, times a godzillion? **Right and wrong, good and bad, POD & POC, all 9, shorts, boys and beyonds.**

Whose lies and what lies am I using to diminish the sexualness I could be choosing? Everything that is, will you destroy and uncreate it, please, times a godzillion? **Right and wrong, good and bad, POD & POC, all 9, shorts, boys and beyonds.**

How much fun and joy and peace have I been avoiding by turning down my sexualness in the face of other people's judgments of themselves and of me? Everything that is, will you destroy and uncreate it, please, times a godzillion? **_Right and wrong, good and bad, POD & POC, all 9, shorts, boys and beyonds._**

"But I'm not really into sex..."

That's okay—you can still function from sexualness, without ever putting your body parts together with somebody else's! If you begin to *be* this energy more and more, and the possibility of copulation from sexualness, rather than sexuality, becomes available to you, you might actually find yourself interested in sex! And if you don't, you are still not wrong!

Once you access and embrace your sexualness, you'll find that it's an unlimited resource and you can direct it where you choose. Okay, the imaginary Q&A over! *Now I'd like to ask YOU something...*

How are you doing with the valuing yourself thing? Is it coming easily for you? A lot of the suggestions I'll make later in this chapter are so much easier to act upon when you have a sense of gratitude for—and honoring of—who you truly are. (And, believe me—I tell you this from experience!)

Once you begin to value yourself, you no longer function from the **need** that drives sexuality (and so many other things!). Getting over that is a huge step towards truly having the freedom to be you and to function from the sexualness that can expand your life in so many ways. Please run this: _What energy, space, and consciousness can I be to be the sexualness I truly be with total ease? Times a godzillion, everything that doesn't allow that, will you destroy and uncreate it, please?_ **Right and wrong, good and bad, POD & POC, all 9, shorts, boys and beyonds.**

A True Gentleman Functions from Sexualness

Friendly reminder: that doesn't mean a true gentleman has to have lots of sex. It means he is allowing himself to BE the ENERGY of sexualness. It all comes back to that either/or thing. I strongly believe that we can be _both_ sexual and gentlemanly.

Just as we can be potent and kind, strong and nurturing, powerful and vulnerable. In fact, a true gentleman functions from sexualness. Sexualness is all about inclusion, about expansion. It broadens your horizons, your experiences, and it enhances your connections with yourself and others.

We have been taught that as men in this world we have to cut ourselves off from our sexualness in order to be respectable, stand-up guys. We have pushed down our desire to connect and we have put a lid on that playful energy, that curiosity that we had as children because now, as adults, the energy of sexualness can be misinterpreted as something else, something more sinister, something 'wrong'.

Please know that **sexualness** is not wrong, or sinister, and it is never threatening.

At the time of writing this book (2017/2018) there are stories breaking all over the media, because it has been reported that more than a few men, in very high-profile positions, have misused their power and influence in order to get women, and men, to sleep with them.

These guys are not functioning from sexualness. They are using their status to get what they want, with no care for their victims, and they are certainly not being healing, caring or nurturing in their actions.

I am bringing this up here, because one potential repercussion of lifting the lid on this conversation could be some guys thinking that by embracing their sexualness they will be like them—misusing their power to get what they want.

Those guys are not gentlemen, and they are not humanoids, seekers or horses. This is the thing that got us into this mess in the first place! Kind, caring, gentlemen like you—being so committed to being kind that you would cut off your sexualness, so that it wouldn't be misconstrued as something totally different that does not honor women *or* men.

Hear this: *You are not wrong because they are.*

You, cutting off your sexualness, simply perpetrates the no-choice sexual reality that we have found ourselves in. You, choosing to be the sexualness that you be, offers a totally different possibility to the world than we have ever seen.

Why Did I Switch It Off?

At this point, some of you may be asking . . . so why on Earth did I switch my sexualness off? One word: *shame.* Okay. I'm going to get a little personal here. Think back to your younger years, all the way back to your teens, maybe even a couple years before. Can you remember those first stirs you felt when you found someone attractive, or when you found a certain situation sexually appealing?

How did that feel? I mean, not physically there in that moment—that felt awesome—but afterwards?

It might have been confusing and disorientating, and if it did it's no wonder—it was all very, very new and, chances are, no one warned you about it. But once the confusion had died down, did you continue to feel really good about these sensations and bodily responses whenever they occurred? Were you totally cool with it, accepting of it? Were you able to talk about it with your parents? Or did something else kick in—some feeling of embarrassment, awkwardness, or shame?

If you were anything like most teenagers on this planet, and if your family operated like so many other families have and continue to do, you might have felt a great deal of shame around the natural and in-no-way-wrong impulse to get to know your body in this way.

Whether it was communicated explicitly or implicitly, you would have sensed and soaked up the message that your body, your sexual energy, and your sexualness is not okay, is not acceptable, and as a result you shut that side of yourself down and switched that energy off. Feelings of wrongness around early sexual exploration is just one example of how the energy of sexualness may have been shamed out of you.

There are a ton of reasons why this happens and why those feelings of wrongness become so strong and feel so real. You might have picked up on the wrongness your parents felt around sexualness, or the feelings and opinions of other family members, your peers, anyone you've ever interacted with, wider society, the media . . .

Are you ready to let that shame go? If so, run this: *Whose lies and what lies have you bought and are you using to make sexualness and having a penis a wrongness, everything that is, will you destroy and uncreate it please,* *times a godzillion?* **Right and wrong, good and bad,** **POD & POC, all 9, shorts, boys and beyonds.**

Run this that as many times as you need to (hint—you may need to run that a few times, or a few hundred times, this is deep, ingrained stuff that we're clearing).

For those of you who have felt a sense of wrongness because your sex drive doesn't seem to match those in your peer group or some of the relationships you've been in, I invite you to run this: *Everything you've done* *to make you wrong for your lack of sex drive, your lack of* *desire for it, or your lack of desire for owning women or* *men, and everything you've done to make yourself wrong* *for your intensely high sex drive, and your desire to own or* *bed everyone and everything, male, female or other, and all* *the lies you have holding all of this in place, will you destroy* *and uncreate it please?* **Right and wrong, good and bad,** **POD & POC, all 9, shorts, boys and beyonds.**

In this reality, we have certainly shut sexualness off, but sexuality, on the other hand...sexuality is somehow accepted as being the norm, celebrated even. And why? Because we've bought into three fairly major myths or limiting points of view around sex. Let's take a look.

Point of View #1: Potency Is All About Getting Laid

And of course, getting laid is proof that you are potent. The more people you sleep with, the more potent you are. If you have slept with more people than the other guys in your peer group, you are the most potent.

Think of the damage that this point of view is doing. If you happen to be a guy who doesn't want to have a lot of sex (or any sex) but you're taking in all these messages that getting laid is a measure of your value as a 'real' man in this world—then you are of course going to perceive yourself as 'less than', wrong and inferior.

Or, if you do want to have sex but you're not getting all that much, for whatever reason—well, again, here you're going to perceive yourself as inadequate. You're going to pile the pressure on yourself; you're going to feel all kinds of—here we go again—*wrong*.

Because, according to this point of view, a successful guy is one who is getting laid. Doesn't matter what kind of sex he's having, what those connections are like—it's all about numbers. Which takes us nicely to ...

Point of View #2: Somebody Wants to Have Sex with Me. I'd Better Comply!

Well, yeah, because you need to keep building on that number, don't you? It doesn't matter if you're not that attracted to her (or him), or you know she (or he) has a boyfriend, or you have a girlfriend, or it's late and you're tired. You just need to keep racking up these sexual encounters because each one deposits a coin into that jar labeled, "I am a real man."

Or—here's another way this one can play out. You're not that guy up there, the one so focused on his magic number. You know that the number of people you've slept with has no bearing on your self-worth. But . . . there's a beautiful, gorgeous siren of a woman giving you all the signs. All the signs. She's so into you, and she tells you. So, you should comply, shouldn't you? Even though you have this niggling feeling that, for some reason that you can't articulate, saying yes might not be the best decision. But, you should still comply, shouldn't you?

Of course you should! So, you sleep with her. Because if you don't, that means you are less of man, according to the sexual judgments of the rest of the world.

Point of View #3: Sex and Desire Are Wrong

Okay, at first this might not make much sense. How can this point of view operate in the same universe as the two we've just explored? How can sex and desire be thought of as wrong if everyone is so focused on them??

A few pages ago I talked about the shame you might have experienced around acting on your early desires. Well, that comes from somewhere.

For me personally, I experienced a tremendous amount of shame from a very young age. I was born male in a family that primarily valued women. I also experienced intense abuse from women who hated men and thought men were the source of all the problems in the world. Even though they were literally beating my body to make the point that men were evil, it never occurred to them that they were perpetrating on me exactly what they said men did to women. Confused much!? The result: a sense of shame and a disconnection from my body, my sexual energy, *and* my sexualness.

And sadly, there are also a lot of messages out there saying that pleasure for pleasure's sake is wrong. It's okay to copulate if it contributes to your magic number, or makes a baby, but embracing the joyful, expansive nurturing energy of sexualness—well no—sorry, not okay.

We could spend time and energy looking at why this has come to be in our world—or we can look at how we get beyond all of this. Focusing on changing other peoples' points of view rarely creates the result we might be looking for. And gentlemen are willing to be things, try things, and do things that others are not.

So, let's talk about how *you*—as the gentleman you truly are—can create something different in your life, and in the world, as a result! Let's talk about how we truly embrace the energy of sexualness. Let's look at some *possibilities!*

New Possibility #1: Potency Is Actually All About Honoring and Valuing You

This one is really simple. I invite you to forget traditional notions of masculinity. You don't need to be the alpha to be powerful, you don't need to dominate all other guys within 50 yards of you to be 'manly', and you don't need to sleep with a lot of women to be potent.

True potency comes when you have a deep, real and genuine appreciation for you as you, when you allow the energy of sexualness to flow freely, and when you let go of all judgments of yourself and others.

When you get to that place, the confidence and ease that oozes from you gives you a power like no other, and it's an easy, comfortable power. It's not about winning, about numbers, about money, about what other people think of you. It's something that comes from you, it emanates from your core, and it opens your world up to amazing, dynamic changes. Other people see it, they sense it, they respond to it.

New Possibility #2: Somebody Wants to Have Sex with Me, but I Can Walk Away!

You absolutely can. The beauty of accepting New Possibility No. 1 into your life is that it brings with it a real understanding that sex, and how much of it you get, is no longer a measure of your worth and allows you to let New Possibility No. 2 into your life.

Remember the example I used a few pages ago of the really hot, attractive and available person who wanted to sleep with you? Who you felt you should say yes to, even though your desire didn't match hers, and even though some part of you knew it wasn't the best choice?

Well, can you imagine actually walking away from someone like that?

Once you know that you are potent and powerful, regardless of whom you sleep with and how often it happens, all kinds of possibilities stem from that realization, and those possibilities include *not* doing certain things.

By the way, please don't think I'm trying to coerce you out of some really amazing experiences—I'm truly not. I'm just suggesting that once you value yourself, you might start making some choices that expand your life—that might seem surprising and far-off to you now.

It took me a really long time to allow this new possibility into my life. I'd meet a woman, I'd be incredibly drawn to her, and I'd know deep within me that sleeping with her was not a choice that would be honoring of me. I would ask myself this question: *Will this create or decay my future?* But even when my instincts said—loud and clear, "This will decay your future! This will decay your future!", so often I just did it anyway. Afterwards, I'd feel odd, and awkward, and like I maybe should have listened more carefully to myself.

That's not to say that was really terrible of me to have those experiences, it wasn't, and there was no need to judge myself as bad for them—but they weren't honoring of me either. And when I did finally walk away from a situation that I knew would not be honoring of me and would only decay my future—*wow! It felt amazing.*

New Possibility #3: Sexualness and Desire Are Allowed, Embraced, Celebrated, and a Gift

Imagine a society where no one was berated for their sexual desires. Where teenagers knew the new pleasures they were having were totally normal, and welcome, and that everyone else had them too, even their parents. And because their parents hadn't flicked the switch to 'off' on their own sexualness, they didn't communicate a feeling of 'wrongness' around the whole thing to their kids. And no one judged anyone else for their sexual orientation, choices, or energy. And we certainly didn't judge ourselves.

Welcome to New Possibility No. 3—*where sexualness is a space of being that is healing, caring, nurturing, joyful, generative, expansive, creative and orgasmic.*

I'd like to invite you, as a gentleman, to really embrace the possibility and potential of this. When a gentlemen functions from their full potential, new possibilities are created, which is something you get to thoroughly enjoy. Amazingly, by being open to it your-self, you invite others to experience joy and sexualness with you.

If you really want to clear the way for the energy of sexualness to enter your life, try this:

Everything you've done to turn off sexualness, to judge it, to have it judged in you, as though you were a bad person if you had it, or as though you were going to turn out to be a bad person, and all the lies creating those points of view, will you destroy and uncreate it please? **Right and wrong, good and bad, POD & POC, all 9, shorts, boys and beyonds.**

Tools for New Possibilities

Let me introduce two key tools that could assist you in stepping into these new possibilities.

Tool 1. Questions to Ask Before Having Sex with Someone

If you recognize yourself from point of view #2: *Someone wants to have sex with me—I'd better comply!* Then you might need a little help stepping into its counterpart: New Possibility #2, otherwise known as, *Someone wants to have sex with me—But I can walk away!*

We've covered the fact that the decision about whether you'll go ahead and have sex with someone is really closely related to whether or not you've embraced the possibility of truly honoring and valuing yourself. So, here are some questions you can ask before making your choice, that will help you have clarity.

1. *Will it be easy?*
2. *Will it be fun?*
3. *Will I learn something?*
4. *Will I be happier afterward?*
5. *Will we both be grateful?*

If you're in a hurry, you can also shortcut all of this with this question: *Will this choice decay or create my future?* I invite you to listen to your awareness, your gut, your instinct—whatever you like to call it—as you ask yourself these questions.

Of course, you might answer 'no' to most of them (or even all of them) and still go ahead and say 'yes'— and no one here is judging you for that, so please don't judge yourself either. It's enough if you can just have the awareness that you haven't been as honoring of yourself as you could have been this time, and be open to the possibility of choosing differently next time.

So, are you willing to choose something different? Are you willing to open yourself up to healing, caring, nurturing, joyful, generative, expansive, creative and orgasmic experiences—that will contribute to you, your life, your energy, and your future? This can also include saying yes to having sex with somebody when it would expand your life! And as you use these questions more and honor you more, you may find that the types of people you choose to have sex with change too! *How does it get any better than that?*

Tool 2. Your Point of View Creates Your Reality

During one of our "Return of the Gentleman" YouTube discussions, Liam and I spoke about how so many more possibilities become available to you as a gentleman when you stop seeing the number of people you've slept with as a means to judge your own value.

I also suggested that when you use the six questions above you will start to choose experiences and women who will enjoy you and be truly grateful for you. Almost immediately several guys responded by saying they had serious doubts that such women exist.

Have you ever felt this way? Have you ever doubted that there are women out there who will enjoy you, and be truly grateful for you? I'd like to introduce you to another tool, but actually it's way, way more than a tool—*it's a shift in how you see the world.*

If you allow it, this shift will contribute to your life in truly phenomenal ways. You should know that it's a really different way of functioning so if you are hearing this for the first time, you might be a bit skeptical at first.

If this happens, I invite you to go with it. We will continue to explore it further as we go through the book, as well. For now, let's dabble in the possibility of it. Let's dabble in the idea that *your point of view creates your reality.*

What I mean by that is—all of your thoughts, feelings, ideas and perceptions create the world you are living in and the experiences that you have.

Reality does not create your point of view; your point of view creates your reality. How does this statement feel to you? Light or heavy?

What would it be like if your thoughts, feelings, language, and perceptions created the world around you and what shows up in your life? If that were the case, then wouldn't it make sense that **you could find different types of partners by changing your point of view**?

Have you ever thought or said something like, "It's so difficult for me to meet women who respect and like me?" Can you consider that this point of view might have an impact on what shows up for you? If we look at what is underneath that statement—it is often more of a point of view that *you* are actually not likeable or valuable.

What if you could change that? This goes back to the conversation of *you* valuing you. When we change our points of view about ourselves, we change our points of view about the world. And then, the world around us surprisingly becomes a very different place!

If you had the point of view that you are valuable, likeable, and a gift to the world (including women), *then* what point of view might you have about who and what can show up in your life? *What amazing things could happen from there?*

Even if it seems really unlikely and really far-fetched that something as simple as changing your point of view could alter your reality, I invite you to try it, and to turn those conclusive, negative thoughts with such finality to them—into something more open, positive and full of possibility.

CHAPTER 6

CREATING NURTURING RELATIONSHIPS

One of the amazing aspects of being a gentleman is that we have the power to create nurturing and meaningful connections with others. This chapter looks at how we can let go of our own limiting points of view, embrace the five elements of intimacy, and go forward into the possibility of truly amazing and fulfilling relationships with everyone around us.

Naturally, a gentleman also has to deal with conflict and resistance, so we'll look at what we can do when such situations arise for us.

The first half of this chapter is focused on building great friendships with the men in our life, while the tools in the second part of the chapter will enrich your interactions with men and women alike.

How a Gentleman Relates to Other Men

Consider once more the origins of this book: that open and enlightening conversation with Liam about how to be a man in this world. Specifically, consider the space in which that conversation took place—not the physical space—but the supportive and nurturing space created and made possible by Liam and me.

Liam spoke from a place of intense vulnerability and intense gratitude, and I allowed myself to receive the gift of Liam, his awareness, and what he was asking for. With no barriers up or walls of judgment around us, the conversation was open and supportive.

In recent years I've had the great, great blessing of friendship from the men in my life who truly have my back. That's the energy I'd like to bring to this chapter. In fact, that's the energy I'd like to run this whole book, and the world!

As gentlemen, I invite you to embrace the possibility of being supportive of, contributing to, and having gratitude for the other men in your life.

Specifically, I invite you to stop seeing other guys as competition, I invite you to have each other's backs, and to let go of any judgments you make based on stereotypes. Let's look at each of those possibilities in more detail.

Stop Seeing Other Men as Competition

This goes both ways, whether you are aware of it or not, there will be guys you view as competition, and there will be guys who view you as competition.

I invite you to let go of any notions of rivalry, any need to prove yourself, any instances of comparing yourself, favorably or unfavorably, to others. _Everything that brought it up, times a godzillion, will you destroy and uncreate it please?_ **_Right and wrong, good and bad, POD & POC, all 9, shorts, boys and beyonds._**

Have you ever felt that intense and separating energy from a certain type of guy who seems to think there are only two very primitive ways to interact with other humans? You know, that throwback to the cavemen days: _mount it or kill it._

Just by virtue of the fact that you are male means you automatically represent competition to that kind of guy (even if you don't feel like you're a particular threat). When you're around someone who really wants to be top of the food chain, you might find they put you into the latter category: _Kill it._

Thankfully, we live in a civilized society. That alpha in the bar, or that particular co-worker in your office, or that friend in your peer group, isn't going to kill you, but his dominating behavior might cause you to make yourself incredibly small when you are around him.

Because you don't wish to match the aggression of guys like this, and because you've always felt a little out of place with how different you are anyway, you might be left with a sense that you don't fit in with other men and that you can't have great connections with them. What if there was a completely different possibility?

We covered this in the early chapters, but it really is worth mentioning again: any disconnections you have felt around other guys, any differences you have in your points of view, behavior, or energy, don't make you less than they are, or wrong in any way.

These differences don't mean that they are wrong either. We can make allowances for these guys as they are, without judgment.

When judgment is out of the equation, everything becomes lighter. You can be around an ultra-competitive alpha, and as a true gentleman—which you are—you can be the most potent guy in the room. *How is this possible?*

What if I said you could cut through all those barriers and walls just by starting a conversation with the guy in question? It really can be that straightforward. The majority of the time, macho competitiveness can be dispelled with something as simple as a handshake and a "Hello."

A small act of kindness can create a big change, and as a gentleman, you can create change like this by introducing the possibility for a new way of relating to other guys, even if they have their barriers up to you.

You may not always get the response you might be looking for when you initiate a shift in the energy—and the key thing to remember here is this; if you choose to have nurturing relationships with other men in your life, you can create that, and it won't depend on anybody specific responding to you in a particular way.

Now, a lot of guys want to have a great relationship with their dad, when in fact their father is not at all nurturing and is actually very caught up in his own judgments. If this is something you've struggled with, I invite you to have allowance for who your dad is, let go of any judgments you have about him or his behavior, and let go of any expectations that it will change.

What has your father shown you by being the man and dad that he is? Even if the only thing you can come up with is that he has shown you *how not to be* a father, you can still be grateful for him.

Have Each Other's Back

I'd like to share a story with you. A little while ago I was in Costa Rica at an Access Consciousness event when I found myself in the men's room at the same time as four other guys, all of whom are part of that valued circle of male friends I mentioned a couple of pages ago.

The five of us were talking about the draining energy of competition, which so often occurs between guys, and how we were all experiencing the negativity of that at the event. During these events, I work with a modality that I've developed called the Energetic Synthesis of Being. It is a way of changing and transforming the very energy we function from that that keeps us stuck in limiting patterns of being.

So, in that moment, I invited these four men to be part of a group session with me . . . It was truly amazing. We unlocked so much of the competition between us that exists for so many men on the planet, and the level of change was phenomenal. It was a moment of awe for all of us.

In the session, we were totally present with each other, contributing to each other, allowing our sexualness to flow, having total gratitude for each other, and we changed the energy of the entire room, which had 150 other people in it. It was a moment of, "Bro, I've got your back," in the truest sense.

It created a palpable change toward more kindness, more caring, and less separation for everyone in the room. Everyone. Men and women alike. And most of them commented on it afterward. Five men, choosing to be true gentlemen with each other, changed 150 people's perception of reality for the greater in an hour. I will always remember, and always be grateful for, what we created together that day.

And if there's anything that I could ask for from writing this book, it would be this: to have all men, all gentlemen, to be that way with each other, to have each other's backs with total vulnerability, total presence, total sexualness, and total joy.

Can you imagine what that could change in the world and what possibilities that would open up? So, my question to you now is: *If you were to embrace that energy, that level of being, vulnerability, potency, and that level of having your own and everybody else's back, what would be possible to change in our world? Everything that doesn't allow you to perceive it, to know it, to receive it and actually to choose to be it now, no matter what it looks like, and no matter what it takes, will you destroy and uncreate it please?* **Right and wrong, good and bad, POD & POC, all 9, shorts, boys and beyonds.**

Forget Stereotypes

What if that beer-drinking, football-watching, loud-talking guy at the bar who looks and acts just like an alpha is actually a really nice guy? What if he can be loud, enjoy a beer, be a sports fan, *and* be kind, caring and nurturing?

It actually doesn't matter so much whether he is a 'nice guy' or not. The key is that we don't make judgments about him because, as we've covered, judgments about anything—ourselves, others, the world around us—limit us and create separation.

I invite you to let go of any judgments you are holding towards other guys, however different you may think you are from them, and in spite of whatever particular energy they bring to the room. Whether you perceive another man to be obnoxious or domineering, or at the other end of the scale—timid or weak, let go of categorizing, and let go of judgments.

Try this: *How many judgments, decisions, conclusions and computations do you have about what a man truly is and what a gentleman is? Everything that is, times a godzillion, will you destroy and uncreate it please?* **Right and wrong, good and bad, POD and POC, all 9, shorts, boys and beyonds.**

When we judge another person, we place them in a box, and once they are in that box it can be hard for us to see that person as anything other than the label we've assigned to them. The same goes for ourselves. This is why I invited you in Chapter 3 (and at various other moments in the book) to let go of any judgments you have of you.

When there are no rights and no wrongs, what else is possible? When you stand in your power as a true gentleman, you can be in a room full of other men who have all placed themselves in competition with you and you can have no issues with that—or them—whatsoever.

When you have let go of all notions of competition and you've let go of all judgments, you can observe that behavior, attitude and energy in others and it can mean nothing to you.

On the other hand—and this is really what makes me excited—when you're in the company of other seekers, you can be a true gift to those fellow gentlemen. Because you're a man who honors himself and others you can create a limitless space for amazing friendships to flourish.

How does it get any better than that?

And Now for Something Completely Different...

Sometimes, the competition that occurs between men is a result of the fact that some guys would actually like to be able to have sex with each other but they can't, and so they turn that energy into anger and competition. This is not easy to acknowledge or accept if you've grown up straight. It's not even easy if you've grown up gay, because there are so many judgments about it.

How does this feel to you, as a possibility? Is it possible that some of the competitiveness you've experienced may be connected to desire? If it feels light, then I recommend you run this:

> *How much of what other men are doing as competition is where they're actually attracted to you or turned on by you and they can't have it, so they have to hate you to keep you far enough away. Everything that brought this up, times a godzillion, will you destroy and uncreate it please?* **Right and wrong, good and bad, POD & POC, all 9, shorts, boys and beyonds.**

These clearings are really useful for allowing the flow of energy to run freely with other guys. Dissolving your previously rigid point of view doesn't mean you're gay, and it doesn't mean you have to have sex with other men. You're simply acknowledging that the energy is there, that it can be there, and that it's okay.

You don't have to shut it off, you don't have to shut those other men out of your life, and you don't have to shut you down. And you don't have to be the effect of their quite-literal desire to fight it.

This awareness came into my world many years ago. Some female friends who do Access Consciousness were out for dinner one night and they saw two guys get in a fight. Because they do Access, they observed the situation, rather than coming to conclusion about it.

They said that it was obvious to them that energetically the guys really wanted to have sex, but they couldn't allow themselves to go there, so they found an outlet for that intense energy and also a way to prove that they didn't have that energy for each other by fighting.

Now, for some of you, this may be a very interesting way of looking at things. In fact, the editor of this book asked me if I wanted to keep it in the book. My answer was yes, because this particular aspect of male-male relationships, especially between men who consider themselves "straight" can be so difficult to understand. And I've found that with more awareness comes more clarity and ease. And for some of you, this particular section was worth the price of the book and your time reading it.

This energy, by the way, is very similar to the energy that creates competition and separation between men. So, if there is a particular man that seems to keep competing with you or trying to bring you down, perhaps he is really attracted to you and is not willing to allow himself to have that energy, so he has to prove that he doesn't have it by creating the energy of fighting you.

The million-dollar question is, *"What do I do about it?"*

1. Start by acknowledging it. By acknowledging it, you come out of the lie that is sticking you. Remember, a lie always makes you heavier. Acknowledging it allows you to perceive what's true, and you get lighter.
2. Next you want to use the *Interesting Point of View* tool from earlier in the book.
3. Then, run these processes to start changing the energy of what is sticking you:

Whose lies and what lies am I using to be at the effect of the unrequited, unacknowledged desire from other men toward me and my body am I choosing? Everything that is, times a godzillion, will you destroy and uncreate it please? **Right and wrong, good and bad, POD & POC, all 9, shorts, boys and beyonds.**

What energy, space, and consciousness can I be to have total clarity and ease with all of this? Everything that is, times a godzillion, will you destroy and uncreate it please? **Right and wrong, good and bad, POD & POC, all 9, shorts, boys and beyonds.**

Remember, this may not change what is going on for them, but it will start to make it easier on you because you are functioning from awareness of what's actually going on, rather than trying to make it about something that it's not.

How a Gentleman Interacts

It's time now to move into the second half of this chapter as we take the spotlight away from the issues that impact male-only friendships and look at how we, as gentlemen, can build nurturing relationships with both men and women in our lives.

So how does one get there? There is one key thing required: **allowing people to have their point of view.** Way back in Chapter 2, I used the 800lb gorilla analogy:

It's not about being the biggest or strongest guy, because when you are being you, you don't have to use force or be intimidating to get your point across.

The 800lb gorilla doesn't have to impose his will on everybody. As a gentleman, you don't claim power by having everyone agree with you. Rather, you get to become two really cool things: *The imposing source for a different possibility* and *the imposing force for a different possibility.*

You allow others to have their point of view. And, if they're choosing a point of view that's limited or hurtful to other people, there's a strong chance that they will naturally move away from the space of possibility you have created. If they don't, you can use the steps in the next section to navigate through any conflicts you find yourself faced with.

Dealing with Conflict as a Gentleman

Conflict occurs when two people have opposing points of view. Even when you become skilled at allowing the point of view of others, you can't stop someone else trying to impose their point of view on you. So how can we, as gentlemen, deal with conflict?

Let's take a more detailed look at how conflict actually works. In any conflict, there are two polarities at play:

The positive polarity: where you agree with a point of view.

The negative polarity: where you resist and react to a point of view.

Let's share an example. It is your roommate's point of view, or the point of view of your wife, or your brother—whomever you live with—that you never take the garbage out. You disagree with this. Your roommate is on the positive polarity (they agree with the point of view) and you're on the negative (you disagree with it).

In this situation you're each stuck on your own side, possibly holding on as tight as you can, and there is no freedom there at all, and there is no way to function from there.

So, how do you deal with a situation like this? The first step in dealing with any conflict is realizing that whenever you disagree with someone else's view, you immediately go into resistance and reaction mode. You resist their point of view, and you react against it.

The key here is to let go of that resistance. Don't resist the fact that this person has this particular point of view, and don't resist that they're fighting for you to agree with them. Resistance really does not help.

Instead of resisting, I invite you to use this Access Consciousness tool: *Interesting point of view. I have this point of view.*

If you're in the midst of conflict with someone right now in an area of your life, I invite you to consider that conflict for a moment. Feel the energy of it, and just say this out loud: *Interesting point of view. I have this point of view.*

Usually, just saying it once shifts the energy a little. One more time: *Interesting point of view. I have this point of view.*

Has it shifted some more?

Interesting point of view. I have this point of view. Interesting point of view. I have this point of view. Interesting point of view. I have this point of view.

Notice those shifts in the energy. By the way, as a true gentleman, you are acutely aware of the energy of every situation you are in, and you're also acutely aware of the energy of every person you're interacting with.

Unfortunately, even though this should set us free and guide us toward greatness, in situations of conflict, it often gets us stuck. If the person we're in conflict with is getting highly agitated, we pick up on that and when we resist it, we become stuck. 'Interesting point of view' acknowledges that there is conflict and allows you to get out of it.

After you've used, 'Interesting point of view', you can ask yourself the following four questions. Again, I invite you to keep a particular conflict in mind, which is present in your life right now as you consider:

> *What is this?* (i.e. *What's really going on here?*)
> *What do I do with it?* (i.e. *How can I handle this?*)
> *Can I change it?*
> And then, if you get a yes answer ... *How do I change it?*

These questions are incredibly useful and allow you to get a different sense of what's actually going on, and what you can do about it.

Acknowledging When You Are Wrong

Is the conflict a result of something you said or did? If you're being truly honest, should you have said or done that thing? Are you willing to apologize? A gentleman is willing to acknowledge when he is wrong, and this can be one of the greatest gifts you can give yourself and the people you interact with.

When we acknowledge we are wrong, something really beautiful happens; we take ourselves out of that place where we were trying to prove that we were right. If you find yourself really holding on to a point of view when you're in conflict with someone, take a moment to pause and look at the effects of holding on so tightly. Would it be so bad to *not* be right?

What if I said you could either be right, or you could be free and happy—what would you like to choose?

Here's how to be free.

You say: *I'm sorry. I was wrong. What can I do to make up for the damage done?* In acknowledging that, you do so with total vulnerability. Here it is again: *I'm sorry, I was wrong. What can I do to make up for the damage done?*

Often, just asking that question opens a door and conflict dissolves. Sometimes, the acknowledgement and apology is all the other person needed. Sometimes, your apology might even shift their point of view. They might come out of their 'right and wrong' way of seeing the situation and acknowledge that neither of you were wrong, you just had two different points of view. That is a really freeing place to be.

Are you always wrong? Not necessarily. Are you always right? Not necessarily. But if you don't have to be right and you don't have to be wrong, you can be totally free.

"Interesting point of view" and *"I'm sorry, I was wrong. What can I do to make up for the damage done?"* are two tools which can create enormous change in your relationships, and I invite you to use them. Recognize that,

as a gentleman, you are the potent person in any situation. In fact, you can be the wizard in the room, *if you choose to be.*

The Five Elements of Intimacy

I believe that intimacy is all about these five ingredients: honor, trust, allowance, vulnerability and gratitude. I also believe that if you function from these five elements you will have meaningful, nurturing, wonderful and expansive relationships with men, with women, and with yourself.

When you, as a gentleman, function from the five elements of intimacy, you are **honoring**, you are **vulnerable**, you have **trust** in yourself and you let other people be who they are. You have a sense of **gratitude,** and you are in **allowance** of anyone you talk to.

Later, in Chapter 8: Charting Your Own Course, we'll look at how you can build on the work you've done to honor yourself by embracing the five elements of intimacy, so you can be intimate with you. Right now, let's look at these elements in relation to our interactions with others.

Honor
Have you noticed how the word 'honor' has come up so many times on the pages of this book? Back in Chapter 3,

we looked at how as gentlemen it's really important that we honor ourselves, and now it's time to go a little wider and take that sense of honoring into our relationships with others.

Simply, when a gentleman interacts with somebody, he's honoring of them. He treats others with regard. This actually makes him stand out because, let's face it, we live in a world where the act of treating others with regard can be hard to come by. Giving someone your time, and being there—being present—with them, is one of the most honoring acts you can do for another.

It really is that straightforward, that beautiful. And that easy. Be totally present for the person you are with and what they are experiencing. Be attentive, and be willing to recognize if you can make a contribution to that person, and if so, if that is something that they can receive from you.

Trust

Trust that whomever you are interacting with is going to show up as they show up—and don't try to change them. Trust that they know what is best for them, even on those occasions when it seems to you that they don't.

I invite you to step away from attempting to make them 'better' or trying to 'improve' them based on what you think might be best for them. That is not honoring of them and the fact that they have choice. True trust requires that you also have allowance: when you trust somebody, you have no judgment, no conclusion, and no point of view about their choices.

Allowance

When you're in allowance of someone, every choice they make is an interesting point of view. There are no right and wrongs, and no judgments. Allowance and judgment cannot exist together, and intimacy is not possible wherever judgment is present.

In fact, going into judgment is like erecting a big wall around you that does not allow you to let yourself or others in to have the very different space of being in the world that true intimacy creates.

Vulnerability

We have been taught to see vulnerability as weakness, and as such, we have been trained to avoid this energy. We don't want to get hurt and we want to appear powerful, so we build walls and barriers around ourselves. Contrary to popular thinking, vulnerability is not weakness—it is actually the greatest potency there is.

When you are truly willing to be with someone with no barriers, you create a different possibility not just for you but also for the person you are with. You can be completely present with them with total allowance and total awareness, and the gift and contribution you can be to somebody from that space is truly phenomenal. Being vulnerable with yourself and others is a space where miracles can begin to occur! And *that*, my friend, is the true potency of being a gentleman!

Gratitude

Gratitude is also a space where judgment cannot exist. *You can either be grateful for someone or something or you can judge someone or something.*

It doesn't matter how another person behaves with you or what their attitude is towards you—in fact, they can be in total judgment of you and you can still be totally grateful for them.

How cool is that? How potent, powerful and expansive is that?

Can you see how all of these elements of intimacy build upon and require each other? You cannot have gratitude without allowance—and when you have gratitude for everything, you have a space of vulnerability that is potent and inspiring.

Trust and honoring can't exist without allowance—and make everything greater in your life and in your relationships. The five elements of intimacy are a space of being that changes the world—and a space that a true gentleman functions from with ease.

With the five elements of intimacy, anything can be created and changed—and without them, well, we are back to the guy we described at the beginning of the book.

On another note, did you notice that there was no mention of copulation in our discussion of intimacy? That's because intimacy has nothing to do with copulation, in contrast to the idea often perpetrated that people who are having sex are "intimate." However, if you chose to be those five elements during copulation, how much more awesome could copulation be?

Recognize the Gift You Are

In Chapter 3, we looked at how acknowledging something, such as noticing where you are already showing up as a gentleman in your life, allows it to grow.

Here I'd like to ask, how do you respond when someone else acknowledges something about you? How easily can you receive that? When someone says you look great, or they really like your sweater, or you're so incredibly funny or thoughtful—how do you respond? How do you receive that?

I ask because in that conversation with Liam, I had a little trouble receiving what he was saying at first. I was surprised that he saw me as an example of how to be a gentleman and I verbalized my surprise with something like, "Whoa really?!"

Often, it's hard to receive gratitude or acknowledgement from someone because we're stuck in a view of ourselves from the past, which is what was happening for me in that moment with Liam. Without being conscious of it, part of me still bought into old beliefs and points of view I held as a young man, or even as a kid.

As a little boy, I felt I had no value, so hearing that I do—and receiving that I do—didn't come easily right away, but once I allowed myself to receive what Liam was saying, it was a real light bulb moment. *Wow!* I thought, *I didn't realize that so much had changed for me!*

So, when you find yourself in those phenomenal and different conversations (and you will), allow yourself to receive what others are acknowledging about you. Would you also be willing to acknowledge that you are a gift? Right now?

You, just by being you, may have a unique possibility to provide something in somebody's world that will change their life for the greater. When you see what another person needs, or what they require, ask yourself if you're willing to provide it. Ask the question, *What will this create in my life, their life, and the world now and in the future?*

If you start functioning from that space, you'll start looking at the world from a different place. Most of us resist what people need. We resist what they desire of us, as though they're somehow taking from us. What if they're not?

What if you have a unique capacity to gift something that will make someone's life greater, only they don't know how to ask for it?

As a gentleman, you have the ability to look for the best in people, and you have the power to bring that out. If you start to embrace this even just a little, you start to recognize the gift that you can be in people's lives and in the world. And If I were to wish one thing for you, it would be just that. Recognize that you are a gift, as you are—right now.

Part Three

Your Future as
a Gentleman

I'd like to invite you to take a moment, a breath, just as we did between Part One and Part Two, to acknowledge where we are, and where we are going.

The focus in Part One of the book fell firmly on us, on recovering and embracing our inner gentleman.

In Part Two, that focus pulled out as we saw how we, as gentlemen, have the ability to embrace our sexual energy and have wonderful relationships and friendships with those around us.

Now, as we move into Part Three, Your Future As a Gentleman, we'll look at how you can be a source of inspiration to the next generation, and how you can utilize your unique power to chart your own course as a gentleman in this world.

Again, in this moment, I invite you to consider:
From here, what else is possible? What else can I create?

CHAPTER 7

RAISING THE NEXT GENERATION

Please note, it is in no way compulsory that you have children of your own in order for you to inspire the younger generation. You don't have to have the constant or even occasional presence of kids in your life in the form of nephews, nieces and so on for you to be a source of guidance to those younger than you.

In fact, your reach as an inspirational force is not even restricted to those who are younger than you—it is totally possible for you to inspire someone who is 20, 30 or 40 years your senior. *How? Because, you are showing a new possibility, a new way of being.*

As a gentleman, you have chosen to be a different kind of man in this reality. That choice alone, that willingness to be different, makes you a leader in this world.

You are a man capable of charting his own course while also being an inspiration to others along the way.

The wonderful thing is, it is actually really easy for a gentleman to inspire others. It happens naturally, with very little effort, and with zero force.

With that in mind, I invite you to consider: *How are you showing up as a source of inspiration for others in your life, right now?*

Toward the end of Chapter 6, I invited you to recognize how you, as a gentleman, can create the possibility for nurturing relationships, and from there be a powerful gift to those around you. Would you like to take a moment to acknowledge that? Remember—acknowledging something makes it grow!

Think of an instance where you were able to contribute to another person's life or day or hour or minute in a positive way. Think of an occasion when you were able to see what someone needed from you, and you were willing to give that something to them.

Here's a quick example from my own experience. A little while ago, while we were staying at a hotel, my young nephew asked if I wanted to play with him. "Sure!" I replied, and we began playing together—which mostly involved the two of us running back and forth through the hotel room over and over.

He had a great time, I had a great time, and the people watching us had a great time. It was pretty simple:

I saw what he required in his world, and I was willing to deliver it. (The video of this encounter made it to my vlog because we had so much fun! And, he gave me his special secret for super-powered running! His secret came as a huge surprise to me, but you have to see the vlog to find out what it was for yourself. By the way, he was five at the time, so it was not some new super-supplement. It was a common, everyday item.)

Seeing what others require from you and making the choice to deliver that—when you can—is one of the ways that you, as a gentleman, can be a gift to others. Please know that you have the power and ability to contribute to and inspire those around you.

The Awareness of Children

As a child, do you remember how you formed your identity? How you gained your sense of self? Did your parent or caregiver present you with all the options of who you could be? Or did they tell you, instruct you, on who you *should* be?

If your upbringing was anything like mine (and a lot of others on this planet) chances are your identity and sense of who you are was formed, or given to you, before you could even talk. Which, when you think about it, is a little messed up because we didn't have the chance to *choose* who we were going to be—or perceive who we actually are, and *be* that!

We just found ourselves being whatever it is that everybody else told us we were, until we got to the point where we wondered what the heck happened, and asked ourselves, "*How did I get here?*"

The answer is that we took our cues from those around us: our parents, our grandparents, our siblings, whoever raised us, or contributed to the raising of us. We picked up on their judgments, their points of view, and their limitations, and began to create ourselves and our lives based on that rather than what is true for and about us.

With that in mind, I invite you to run this: <u>*How many projections, expectations, separations, judgments and rejections did I pick up in my Mom's world, my Dad's world, the other men in my life, and the other women in my life, that have defined who, what, why, when and who I am as a man and a gentleman and who, what, why, when and who I am not, and cannot be as a man and a gentleman? Everything that is, times a godzillion, will you destroy and uncreate it please?*</u> ***Right and wrong, good and bad, POD & POC, all 9, shorts, boys and beyonds.***

What we have to realize, when it comes to raising our own children, or interacting with any of the kids in our lives—those nephews, nieces, family friends: **is that they are aware.**

Often, we assume awareness is something that kicks in when kids become adults. Not so. Children are aware from the time they are born. Think about how a tiny baby knows that a particular cry at a certain pitch will grab their parents' attention in a heartbeat. Even before language, a baby has awareness.

One of the greatest gifts we can give to any young person is to acknowledge that they have awareness. This lays the foundation for acknowledging the gift that they are, and from there the possibilities of who they could be. Whether you are a parent, caregiver, uncle, teacher or friend—this is an amazing gift to give to someone.

Inspiring the Next Generation

How can we be with the children in our lives? What can we show those kids who look up to us?

First, understand that children look to grown-ups for guidance. They look to us to model behavior. Although the discussion in this chapter is applicable to raising boys and girls, it's useful here to acknowledge and realize the impact we, as gentlemen, can have on the boys and young men in our life.

We can model our behavior (that sounds somewhat artificial, when in fact it's something very natural) in such a way that we can show these young guys the possibility of how they can be and what they can create—and we do this just by being ourselves.

So, simply and beautifully, if you are being the true gentleman that you are, if you are being all those elements that we've discussed so far in the book, if you are honoring yourself, honoring others, if you are in allowance and out of judgment, then you are already showing the young men in your life a tremendous amount of possibility. You are already contributing to them being something greater in this world.

Let's go a little deeper, get a little more specific, and look at the particular gifts that we as gentleman can give the children in our lives.

Gift 1: Freedom

When we give our kids the freedom to make mistakes, we give them one of the greatest gifts they will ever receive in their lives. And, if we don't make them wrong when they make a mistake, even when they choose something that seems to us to be a colossal failure, then we are truly giving them the freedom to choose for themselves, *and to know that they will not be made wrong for their choices.*

If you look back on your own childhood, were you ever made wrong for any of the choices you made? Maybe you were made to feel wrong because you chose to not study as hard as your father thought you should—or maybe you studied harder than anyone in your family previously had and that was seen as wrong and weird. Maybe your mom didn't approve of the time you got up in the morning, or the friends you chose to hang out with, or the clothes you wore.

Or something bigger, like your sexuality, or something smaller like how often you washed your hair. If any of that is relevant to you—run these clearings:

Everywhere I have been made wrong dynamically for the choices I've made, even made so wrong I don't want to make choices anymore, destroy and uncreate it all please? **Right and wrong, good and bad, POD & POC, all 9, shorts, boys and beyonds.**

Whose lies and what lies am I using to create the perpetual wrongness of me I am choosing? Everything that is, times a godzillion, will you destroy and uncreate it please? **Right and wrong, good and bad, POD & POC, all 9, shorts, boys and beyonds.**

When we allow children the freedom of their own choices, we are operating in total allowance for them. Remember how allowance and judgment cannot exist side by side? Well that leads us nicely to...

Gift 2: No Judgments

The platform for giving our children the freedom to mess up is having no judgments about any of their choices. Because, quite simply, it's our judgment of our kids that messes them up, makes them feel like they're wrong, or makes them doubt themselves. And we don't have to do that. We're bigger than that, and we have different tools than that. We have the ability and capacity to create a different possibility for them.

Ask questions. Ask your kids, *"What's going on for you?"* And here is one thing that cannot be overestimated—make time for them if they're desiring that time. Create time where you are in total allowance of them. Do not judge them no matter what they bring up.

Did your parents judge you? If they did, just as mine did, how did that work out for you? When we are judged by our parents, we often go into resistance and reaction to them—which diminishes the gratitude and joy in our own lives. Judgment kills creativity and possibility—and kids are very aware of that even before they are verbal. Do we want to do that to our kids?

This is a really key point: If you can consider how to create something greater for others than you have had for yourself— then you are a true gentleman.

A gentleman looks and sees how he can actually make a moment, a situation, the whole world, greater for everyone, even if it's greater than what he himself had.

As gentlemen, we realize that bringing that greatness into the world allows it to exist in the world, which in turn allows us to create a greater world.

Consider this: How do you make the world greater for everybody, even when you yourself were never gifted that possibility? ***What if you treated kids (and adults, and everyone else) the way you should have been treated, not the way you were treated?***

Gift 3: Be Willing to Be Vulnerable

In the same way that your kids look to you for guidance, you can look to them for guidance too. You can learn from your kids in the most wonderful, rich, and unexpected ways.

If we allow ourselves to acknowledge this, we can acknowledge the occasions where we need to be the leader, as well as the occasions where we can learn something from them.

Please note that while vulnerability allows us to be honest with our children, it's not a reason to burden them with our problems. We can tell them we have stuff going on in our lives, that we're not perfect, *and* that we are willing to do all we can to make their world a better place.

As gentlemen, we don't always have all the answers. We are willing to receive contributions from anywhere they might exist in the world, including from our kids or the younger people in our lives. We realize it is a gift to learn from other people, and we are willing to be vulnerable enough to acknowledge this and be grateful for it.

If that lesson comes to you from your six-year-old—know that they probably learned whatever they are teaching you *from you* in the first place. Acknowledge that, too, not from a place of arrogance, but from a place of realizing what a gift you are.

Vulnerability is also about knowing when you are wrong, and when you've messed up. We all do it. None of us are perfect, and occasionally we're going to say or do something out of line around our kids. I'd like to invite you to accept that and know its okay. *If you don't have to be perfect, what other choices do you have?*

Are you willing to be wrong around your kids? Can they be right, and you be wrong? Try running this: *Everywhere I'm not willing to mess up, and everywhere I'm not willing to be wrong, destroy and uncreate it please? Times a godzillion.* **Right and wrong, good and bad, POD & POC, all 9, shorts, boys and beyonds.**

Brendon and Nash

I'd like to tell you about my great, and dear friend, Brendon, and his awesome son, Nash. At the time of writing, Nash is twelve years old. As a father, Brendon has truly given the three gifts above to Nash. Nash has the freedom to make his own choices, and whatever choices he makes he is never wrong, and he's also never right. He just is who he is, and his dad never judges him for that, or for his choices.

When Nash comes to Brendon with a particular problem, Brendon has a really useful set of questions which he uses to guide his response. Here they are:

If this were me, how would I like this to be dealt with?
If this were me at his age, what would I have heard?
And what would have helped change it for me?

So again, this is all about how we, as gentleman, can create something greater for others, greater than what was created for us.

As a dad, Brendon functions from a place where he is totally willing to be wrong and to mess up. He is willing to be vulnerable, and that vulnerability allows him to acknowledge when he makes a mistake, apologize, and ask Nash where they can go from there. The space and possibility created by this is really phenomenal, and I invite you to use this approach with the children and young people in your life.

Ultimately, Brendon realizes that Nash is looking to him for guidance, to show him the way, to show him what was possible. And the simple and awesome truth is that Nash is a great kid because Brendon has, just by being who he is, created an invitation for his son to be who he actually is. Parenting is not about teaching, *but about being*. This is the gift that you are.

Talk About Mom with No Point Of View

If you're no longer with the mom of your kids, or if you're still together, but the relationship isn't in a good place, be aware of how you speak about her. Simply put, *when you talk about Mom, talk about Mom with no point of view*.

When a difficult situation arises, ask questions rather than sharing judgments about her. Here are some examples:

How was that for you?
When Mom said that, how did that make you feel?
Was that lighter or heavier?
Did you feel more of you, or did you feel less of you?
Did you feel more happy, or did you feel less happy?

Realize that your kids are going to do everything they can to play Mom against you, and you against Mom. It doesn't mean they're bad kids; it's just what kids learn to do. They will take any opportunity to manipulate anybody they can.

If that sounds at all familiar, here's what you want to run: <u>*What energy, space and consciousness can I be to totally out manipulate my kids (or all kids) for all eternity*</u>

with total ease? Everything that doesn't allow it, **Right and wrong, good and bad, POD & POC, all 9, shorts, boys and beyonds.**

A New Generation, a Different Possibility

Please realize that you have created—or that you can create—a different reality than the one you were handed as a child. Moreover, as a gentleman you can create a different possibility for the future for the young men and women on the planet. You are as powerful, as able, and as potent as that.

Once we start to really understand this, to embrace even a tiny bit of it, and to realize that it's a possibility as a way of living, then we start to change our entire dynamic of how we function with ourselves and with each other, and we start to change the entire dynamic of people interacting on this planet. *How does it get any better than that?*

CHAPTER 8

———

CHARTING YOUR OWN COURSE

So here we are, gentlemen—in the final chapter of the book—and what a journey it has been to get here. From recovering our inner gentleman, to letting him out into the light, to embracing so many new possibilities in how we be as ourselves and how we be with others, to recognizing that we are a source and a force for possibility for everyone on the planet.

We're not even done yet! I still have more to share with you, and I'm especially excited about this chapter, because there's so much freedom and possibility in what we're about to discuss. In this final chapter, the focus is back on us; the greatness in our being gentlemen, and how we get to chart our own course.

Functioning from Creation

What does creation mean to you, as a gentleman? Is creation about sex? Is creation *only* about sex? What if creation is actually about so much more than sex?

We've talked a lot about how we, as gentlemen, have the ability to let go of any need for outside validation, and how we no longer need to 'prove' ourselves through our sexual conquests, or our perceived attractiveness.

If, in the past, you have defined your creativity based on sex and having sex with those who are attracted to you, you may find that when you actually begin to really sense and understand the energy of creation, the need for sexual validation dissolves. This is a really amazing place to be. How does that sit with you?

Try running this: *How much have you misidentified and misapplied that creation occurs through sex, and creation only occurs through sex? Everything you did to buy that, and everything that creates the guy you're supposed to be, rather than you getting to be the gentleman you could truly be—which is actually not just a guy—but somebody who has all aspects of sexualness available, and all aspects of creation available; will you destroy and uncreate it please? Times a godzillion.* **Right and wrong, good and bad, POD & POC, all 9, shorts, boys and beyonds.**

The journey we have been on has taken us beyond judgment and wrongness to a place where we can create our own reality. We no longer have to accept the realities imposed upon us. Simply, wonderfully and expansively, we chart our own course.

How to Honor Everyone without Losing You

We first explored the five elements of intimacy (honor, trust, allowance, vulnerability and gratitude) in Chapter 6. Back then, we looked at how we could function from these elements to create nurturing relationships with others. Now, I invite you to dive deeper into using these elements, to have true intimacy with yourself.

Honor *You*

At the risk of sounding repetitive, here it is again; you can honor yourself by making choices which honor you. Choose what you really desire, not the thing you're supposed to want. If this still feels difficult or blurry for you, you can call on this tool from Chapter 3.

Before you make a choice, ask yourself, "*Will this be honoring me?*" And, if you're not sure, use the 'light or heavy' question to help guide you. Simply, does doing the thing you are considering feel light or heavy for you?

Trust *You*

The one thing that will really allow your life to work brilliantly and allow you to go where you know you need to go (even if nobody else follows) is cultivating a trust in you. When you trust yourself, you no longer look outside of you for what you need, or for confirmation that you're making a good choice for you.

> *What if you're the only one who knows what's true for you?*
> *What if you're the one you can trust to create what you desire in life?*

Be in Allowance of *You*

When you're in allowance, everything you choose is just an interesting point of view. There are no rights and no wrongs. There are no judgments.

Think of something you have judged yourself for. It could have occurred in the last week, the last ten years, maybe even further back in your past. It may have been an action, an incident, something you said or did. Feel the energy of that. Now take that energy and use one of the tools we explored in Chapter 6: *Interesting point of view. I have this point of view.* In Chapter 6, we used this tool when in conflict with others. How about using it when we're in conflict with ourselves?

Think about that incident and say (out loud, if you can), "Interesting point of view. I have this point of view." Repeat this a few times if you need to. As a gentleman, fixed points of view are not for you. Feel the energy shift. You can practice this allowance with anything that is sticking for you.

Be Willing to Be Vulnerable with *You*

Being vulnerable means having no walls and no barriers up whether we are with a group of people, one other person, or by ourselves. Functioning from a place of vulnerability means we have no need to prove anything.

It's so easy for guys in this reality to feel that they have something to prove. They try to prove that they're macho, they're not afraid, they have it all together, they're sexy, valuable, desirable...

A hallmark of a gentleman is that he has nothing to prove. When you allow yourself to be vulnerable, you give yourself the freedom to make mistakes. You do not need to be perfect, and you absolutely have nothing to prove.

Have Gratitude for *You*

What would it be like if you had gratitude for you every single day? If you were grateful for the life you have created so far; for your willingness to change, and to choose something different? And, you were grateful for what makes you uniquely you? Recognize the gift of you, as you are.

To truly embrace functioning from the five elements of intimacy, I invite you to run this: *What energy, space and consciousness can I be to have total allowance, honoring, trust, vulnerability and gratitude for me and my body for all eternity? Everything that doesn't allow it times a godzillion, destroy and uncreate it please?* **Right and wrong, good and bad, POD & POC, all 9, shorts, boys and beyonds.**

True intimacy with you is one of the greatest gifts you can give yourself, and the world, as a gentleman. It substantiates brilliantly so many of the concepts we've discussed in the chapters up to this point. When you have intimacy within you, you are the consummate gentleman. You value yourself, you recognize your potency, you see what a gift you are, and others follow suit.

Choice—the Source of Everything

This whole process starts with choice. When you are willing to choose something different, an abundance of doors open up to you. It is as simple and as beautiful as that.

Remember those lines from the prologue? Okay, you may not—it was thousands of words ago, and you have come so far since then.

Can you recognize how, just by still being here, reading these words which form the final chapter of this book, you have chosen and embraced a new way of being? Can you acknowledge your willingness to choose something different, and your openness to all the possibilities this choice entails?

It's no surprise to me, my friend—you're a seeker, after all.

Let's spend a moment mapping out our journey to here to really acknowledge how far we have come. From the start of the book to this moment...

Have you chosen to let go of...?
The boxes and roles of being a man that hold
    you back
Any sense that you are 'wrong' just for being male
Any sense of how you *should be,* or who you
    should be
Traditional notions of masculinity and femininity
Concepts of *either* and *or*
Separation from men, women... and you
Judgment—of yourself and of others

Have you embraced the possibility of...?
Honoring and valuing yourself
Being vulnerable, messing up, and letting in a
    lighter, more joyful side of you
Being gentlemanly *and* sexual
Being grateful for the other men in your life

Have you recognized that . . . ?

As gentlemen, we are creators; we can create change

We can choose to create something for others, even when it is more than what was created for us

Our point of view creates our reality

And to bring us right up to speed, can you recognize that:

As a gentleman, you chart your own course.

Observer or Creator?

How involved, how active, *how creative* are you when it comes to living your life? Are you very much in the driving seat? Are you at the helm of the ship? Or, are you taking a backseat? Are you hanging out on the observation deck, at the mercy of everything around you?

One of the amazing gifts of being a gentleman comes when we become aware that it is within our power, not just to participate in your reality, but to also create your reality. As gentlemen, as seekers, as horses—we were not made to sit back and have life happen to us. We are the agents of change. This takes us back to a concept I touched upon in Chapter 5: *Your point of view creates your reality.*

This means all of your thoughts, feelings, ideas and perceptions create the world you are living in, and the experiences that you have. Reality does not create your point of view; your point of view creates your reality.

How amazing is that? How exciting, expansive, open, and freeing is that?

If we get to create our own reality, then we really do have the capacity to initiate amazing change, to be the wizard in the room, and to be the force and source for new possibilities in our own lives and in the lives of those around us. Again, I have to ask you: *How amazing is that?*

Ask and You Will Receive

Since you started making certain choices, since you have opened yourself up to new possibilities, are you willing to embrace this?

The Universe is on your side. The Universe wants what is best for you, and is simply waiting for you to ask for it.

If you function from this train of thought, you can really start to put the notion of, *Your point of view creates your reality,* into action; and you begin to experience the true power of being you. How mind-blowingly thrilling is it *to be that?!* Here's how you can ask the Universe for what you would like to show up in your life.

First, feel the energy of that thing by getting the sense of what it would be like to have it. It might be a relationship, an experience or an object—or a combination of all of these, or something else entirely; something you wish to be, to do, or to have.

Tell the Universe this is what you are doing. Say, "I am sensing the way it would be for me to be this, or do this, or have this," and add, "Universe, I'm asking for this." This acknowledgment makes it really clear between you and the Universe that you're asking for whatever it is you desire.

Next say, "Consciousness, Universe—**hook a brother up please.** I don't know how it's going to happen, but I'm willing to be or do anything to make this happen. I'm willing to change anything to have this happen."

That's it. Done. And then you live your life. You don't need to concern yourself with how it will happen for you, but when you get the sense of something that feels like that energy you conjured—head in that direction.

Believe me, from my experience of working with hundreds of thousands of people around the world, I can tell you that if you make a choice about something, if you ask the Universe for it, you'll find a way to get there—even when you have no cognitive idea how to get the thing, the relationship, the experience. When you make the choice for it, the pathway appears. That's how potent you are!

Nothing to Lose but Your Limitations

I tell you this from my own personal experience. You have nothing to lose but your limitations. This might resonate with you, if you have a certain reluctance towards making decisions or choosing a particular direction.

Often, the biggest thing that people are most concerned about, or afraid of losing, is actually their place in this reality. This exact thing happened to me.

Several years ago, I was in Italy with my friend Gary Douglas, when I woke one particular morning feeling pretty sad and depressed. The previous night, Gary and I had done some processing, which had unlocked some major limitations for me. Yet, there I was, the next day, feeling awful—so blue, and so low. Gary asked what was wrong, and all I could say was that I was sad. I asked for his help, and he began asking questions to try to uncover whatever it was that was going on with me.

Each time he asked a question, I answered with, "I don't know," until he said, "Do you feel like you're losing something?"

"Yes, it's exactly that," I said.

"So, what have you lost?"

Then came the answer: "Oh, my limitations!"

I started laughing. I realized that all I had lost was this major segment of my limitations in the world. It was such a freeing moment when that realization came to me.

Does any of that feel possible for you? Might you be afraid of losing what is actually holding you back? If this feels like you, run this: <u>*What have I made so vital, valuable, and real about the "loss" of limitations that keeps me forever lamenting rather than choosing the joy & freedom I truly be? Everything that is, times a godzillion, will you destroy and uncreate it please?*</u> **<u>Right and wrong, good and bad, POD & POC, all 9, shorts, boys and beyonds.</u>**

And then run it again. And again.

Who Would You Be without Your Limitations?

I believe that you truly have the capacity to change reality as we know it. You have a power within you, whether you have realized that yet or not.

As a gentleman, you get to be it all; you empower people, you have fun, enjoy sex, enjoy male friends, female friends, and you enjoy creating. Your life just works. You're being everything you are. You're the person willing to say yes, willing to say no, willing to be wrong, to mess up, to see what's required for the future, to acknowledge whether you're willing to go there, and create what you came into this world to create.

You are somebody who can handle any situation.

You are a gift to yourself and everyone in your life. You present a new possibility for a way that we can be in the world together. You show others that separation is not necessary. You show others that hatred need not exist, and that sexualness can exist; that joy can exist.

You are an invitation to a reality where it is actually okay to have a good time, to have money, to be sexual, to be vulnerable, to feel good about yourself, to be proud of yourself, to be proud of what you're creating, and be proud of inviting other possibilities.

You have pride in the difference about you. Not an arrogance about the difference, but a pride in it. You have pride in the fact that you get to be the greatness that you are, which invites others to be the greatness that they are. And this pride in the difference about you often, contrary to popular belief and dogma, actually leads to a humble gratitude for the gift you get to be.

You see the possibility to change anything into something greater, and you choose that. You have no idea whether the choice that you make today will influence and reach others, yet you choose today to be potent, kind, brilliant, generous, curious, and vulnerable. And you are willing for that choice to change the face of our entire future.

Once you truly recognize that your future is in your hands, ask yourself:

What will I choose?

What can I choose to create that's never been created before?

What can I choose and create that's never been asked for before?

What else is possible?

I invite you to engage in life and living in a way that makes you excited to bound out of bed every day, ready to create.

I invite you to be the gentleman that you are, and to embrace and relish all of the gifts that you will receive by being you, and all of the gifts you can offer to the world by being you. What if you, truly being you, is exactly the gentleman that this world requires?

Really.

THE BEGINNING

How can I round up this process, this journey, *this joyous ride*?

How can I end the book, which is really just the beginning? I will do my best by offering a few not-so-final thoughts. Let me start by saying that, yes, this is the end of this book—and the *very beginning of the rest of your life.*

THIS IS WHEN YOUR JOURNEY REALLY GETS STARTED:

Do you recall the snapshot of a scene I asked you to imagine at the very start of this book, that moment where you, as a gentleman, could look in the mirror and really like the guy looking back at you? Were you were truly grateful for you and the greatness that you are, with no judgment, no shame and no apology? As appealing as it sounded, did it also feel selfish, far away, even impossible, back then?

What about now?

Are you able to take a moment to acknowledge how far you have come from the first time you considered that mirror-moment? I invite you to step into the energy of where you are right now—of all you have let go of, embraced, recognized and created; all you have chosen.

Acknowledge everywhere you've previously tried to fit in. You are now willing to tread alone as a gentleman—as a leader whose validation no longer comes from others, *but from yourself.*

Acknowledge, not only the choices you have made to get to here, but the possibilities of the choices *still to be made* now that you have returned to the gentleman that you are.

From the genesis of this book, to this moment right here, it remains one of my greatest hopes that the sharing of this conversation will open up the dialogue around being a man in this reality for as many guys as it is possible to reach.

If the process of reading and sharing this journey with me has opened doors for you, if you have experienced any light-bulb moments, if you have sensed or are experiencing the amazing changes that come from being a true gentleman, I would love for you to share this book—and have this conversation—with the men in your life who are willing to receive it.

Life is a roaring, thrilling, kick-ass journey; go on the ride. Be the agent of change.

Enjoy creating your life as the *gentleman you truly be*, my friend.

ABOUT THE AUTHOR

International speaker and author **Dr. Dain Heer** travels all over the world facilitating advanced classes on Access Consciousness. He invites and inspires people to more consciousness from total allowance, caring, humor and a phenomenal knowing.

Dr. Heer started work as a Network Chiropractor back in 2000 in California, USA. Having worked with bodies since he was in college, he came across Access Consciousness at a point in his life when he was deeply unhappy and even planning suicide. Access Consciousness changed all of that.

While none of the other modalities and techniques Dr. Heer had been studying were giving him lasting results or change, with Access Consciousness his life began to expand and grow with more ease and speed than even he could have imagined possible.

Today, Dain Heer is best known for his powerful energetic transformation process, called The Energetic Synthesis of Being™, and for being the co-creator of Access Consciousness, along with the founder, Gary Douglas. Dr. Heer has a completely different approach to healing by teaching people to tap into and recognize their own abilities and knowing. The energetic transformation process is fast—and truly dynamic.

A conscious and creative thought leader with a profound understanding of the power of personal creation, Dr. Heer draws upon his background and unique perspective to facilitate positive change in the world, and empower people from every culture, country, age and social strata to create the money, relationships and life they truly desire.

Find out more about Dr. Dain Heer on **drdainheer.com**.

ABOUT ACCESS CONSCIOUSNESS

Access Consciousness is available in more than 170 countries and has contributed to changing the lives of tens of thousands of people around the world for the past 30 years. Delivered through seminars, teleseries, books, audios and consultations, what most people love about it is that it actually works!

Access Consciousness is an ever-evolving energy transformation program which offers you the tools and questions to create everything you desire in a different and easier way, and to change the things in your life that you haven't been able to change until now.

Access is based on the idea that you're not wrong, that you know and that consciousness can shift anything. It provides you with ways to become totally aware and to begin to function as the conscious being you truly are. It gives you access to the possibilities that exist when you no longer stick yourself and no longer believe that you are stuck. If you had total choice available, what would you create?

- *If your purpose in life were to have fun, what would you change?*

- *If you were celebrating your life today, what would you choose?*
- *What else is possible that you've never considered?*

The aim of Access Consciousness is to create a world of consciousness and oneness. Consciousness includes everything and judges nothing. Consciousness is the ability to be present in your life in every moment, without judgment of you or anyone else. It is the ability to receive everything, reject nothing, and create everything you desire in life—greater than what you currently have, and more than what you can imagine.

The information, tools and techniques presented in this book are just a small taste of what Access Consciousness has to offer. There is a whole Universe of processes and classes. Although these tools have generated a great deal of change in the lives of many people, Access Consciousness does not declare itself to be the only way. Access empowers you to know what is true for you. It allows you to know that you know!

If there are places where you can't get things in your life to work the way you know they ought to, then you might be interested in attending an Access Consciousness class or workshop or locating a facilitator. They can work with you to give you greater clarity about issues you haven't yet overcome.

Find out more on **accessconsciousness.com**

OTHER BOOKS BY DAIN HEER

Dr. Dain Heer is the author and co-author of 12 books, many of them translated into several languages.

Being You, Changing the World
The Baby Unicorn Manifesto
Embodiment
Magic. You Are It. Be it.
Right Riches for You
Talk to the Animals
Sex Is Not a Four-Letter Word,
    but Relationship Oftentimes Is
Living Beyond Distraction
The Ten Keys to Total Freedom
Money Isn't the problem, You Are
Home of Infinite Possibilities

Through the Access Consciousness shop online you can find these and many other books that will allow you to dive deeper into different possibilities in areas like money, relationships, kids, addiction, bodies, grief, leadership and more.

Turn the page to a different possibility on
accessconsciousness.com/shop